Labouring Lives

'Archana Aggarwal has written a book that every student of Indian capitalism will want to read. Brilliantly weaving together economic analysis with ethnographic observation and interviews, she makes a highly complicated phenomenon simple to digest. Abstract categories are given flesh and bone, suffusing the book with great sympathy without sacrificing analytical rigour. A most impressive achievement.'
VIVEK CHIBBER
New York University

'This short book tells the grim story of how India, through successive economic regimes, creates very few, highly exploitative and primarily low paying jobs. Weaving together stories of the lived experience of workers, Archana Aggarwal tells us how this condition, even in advanced sections of manufacturing, creates a situation where workers are so fearful of job loss and victimisation that it intimidates them into not joining a trade union. At a time when workers' rights are being written down, it leaves the reader with the raw question – what might the way forward be?'
GAUTAM MODY
New Trade Union Initiative

Labouring Lives
Industry and Informality in New India

Archana Aggarwal

First published in May 2023

LeftWord Books
2254/2A, Shadi Khampur
New Ranjit Nagar
New Delhi 110008
INDIA

LeftWord Books and Vaam Prakashan are imprints of
Naya Rasta Publishers Pvt. Ltd.

leftword.com

ISBN   978-93-92018-04-6 paperback
          978-93-92018-05-3 ebook

Digital print edition, July 2024

Visit website

In memory

Contents

Abbreviations

CAGR	Compound Annual Growth Rate
CPC	Central Pay Commission
CSE	Centre for Sustainable Employment
CT	Company Trainee
DMIC	Delhi Mumbai Industrial Corridor
DT	Diploma Trainee
EOI	Export Oriented Strategy of Industrialization
ESI	Employees' State Insurance
ESIC	Employees' State Insurance Corporation
FDI	Foreign Direct Investment
FTE	Fixed Term Employment
GATWU	Garment and Textile Workers Union
GDP	Gross Domestic Product
GPN	Global Production Network
GVA	Gross Value Added
GVC	Global Value Chain
H&M	Hennes & Mauritz
IDA	Industrial Disputes Act
ILO	International Labour Organisation
IMT	Industrial Model Township
IR	Industrial Relations Code
ITI	Industrial Training Institute
MSIL	Maruti Suzuki India Limited
MSME	Micro, Small, and Medium Enterprises
MSWU	Maruti Suzuki Workers Union
MUL	Maruti Udyog Limited
NAS	National Accounts Statistics
NCLR	National Commission on Rural Labour

NCR	National Capital Region
NCT	National Capital Territory
NEEM	National Employment Enhancement Mission
NPA	Non-Performing Assets
NSS-EUS	Employment-Unemployment Surveys of National Sample Survey
OEM	Original Equipment Manufacturers
OSHWC	Occupational Safety, Health and Working Conditions
PLFS	Periodic Labour Force Surveys
PMKVY	Pradhan Mantri Kaushal Vikas Yojana
PMP	Phased Manufacturing Program
PUDR	Peoples Union for Democratic Rights
RUPE	Research Unit for Political Economy
SSI	Small Scale Industries
ST	Student Trainee
VMC	Vertical Machine Control

List of Illustrations

Foreword

Amit Bhaduri

Economics is a puzzling subject because it operates at different levels. At one level, it is 'high theory', increasingly dominated these days by sophisticated mathematical and statistical techniques. It is an area reserved for those with professional training, but if the uninitiated layman or woman hopes to gather a deeper understanding from it about the real world, she would mostly be sadly disappointed. The emperor has no clothes, and the mathematical sophistry often based on absurdly unreal assumptions does not yield fruitful results for understanding real-life happenings. It is dominated by techniques rather than insights and, often worse – a justification of the mythical world of a perfectly functioning market economy. At best only minor blemishes of the market mechanism are discussed, like a failure of the market to function perfectly due to imperfect knowledge. In contrast, more important issues about how economic power is acquired and used to manipulate markets and other institutions of governance are avoided.

Not surprisingly, economic theory at this level has increasingly failed to deliver anything of substance that a non-economist can appreciate, except repeating the message that 'more free market-oriented reforms' and more austerity for government spending are virtues in all situations. Its somewhat precarious respectability as an academic discipline continues today in a patron-client relation. Multilateral agencies fund research in universities and institutes, and large bank and corporations award academic prizes advertized as 'good research' worth emulating. Some well-intentioned professional economists are aware of this state of affairs but can do little to change the system. So, they often tend to engage in empirically oriented research that allows the use of more sophisticated statistical techniques even if the data does not always justify it. This, too, is largely technique-driven empirical research meant for acquiring respectability, not new knowledge. Moreover, there is nothing called pure empirical research without theory in either framing the questions or interpreting the results.

And yet, there is the third level where the purpose is to seek an explanation from direct observation. When you look at data to reconsider received wisdom of economic theory or try to formulate new ideas, not necessarily a statistically testable hypothesis. It involves not only collecting data but also impressions from direct interaction with those living the experience of industrialization through land acquisition, market reforms for small business, new labour laws for the contract workers and so on. The aim is to obtain a coherent picture, and many such pictures together provide an analytical description of the state of the economy.

There are not many who have viewed this process systematically from below. It is a kind of subaltern economics, a narration by people directly affected buttressed with data for wider relevance. The meaning of expressions like 'global supply chain', the distinction between 'living wage' and market wage, economic insecurity and similar ideas that appear in the abstract in learned policy discussions become concrete with suffering human faces for the reader. This little book is a step in that direction, a greatly welcome step because it helps us to connect economic analysis with reality. The greatest virtue of this book is to imprint firmly in our mind that policy involves people, especially vulnerable groups of people in labouring India. And once the reader becomes acutely aware, she would find it so much easier to distinguish fact from fiction and even choose sides. This wonderfully written book that goes to the heart of many economic policy issues will be equally educative for the specialist as well as the non-specialist reader because it bridges the gap between what we know and what we should know but usually do not know. I hope it will be very widely read.

Delhi, March 2023

Preface

The journey of a manuscript is also the journey of its author, a fragment and a mirror of one's intellectual and political life. I engaged with economics for the first time as an undergraduate student in 1984, hoping that the discipline would enable me to make sense of our society. A few years later, some friends helped me understand that society is more layered and complicated than my young mind initially fathomed. Teachers and mentors at the Centre for Economic Studies and Planning (CESP), Jawaharlal Nehru University, provided the tools to understand the scope and the limitations of conventional economics.

Fast forward to the 2000s. I had been teaching economics to undergraduate students for more than a decade. I started *Perspectives*, an informal research group in Delhi University, along with some like-minded students. We interviewed farmers in Punjab and Maharashtra to understand the agrarian situation and the incidents of farmer suicides. We met workers in the peripheries of metropolitan Delhi to understand how industrial policy impacted them. Over seven years and several summer and winter vacations, this work took us to villages and factories, offices of automobile companies, and initiated conversations with many academics, policymakers and activists. I continued my visits even after the *Perspectives* experiment ended in 2014. I travelled to Gurgaon, Noida, and Manesar, to the homes of workers and their factories, sometimes with my students and sometimes by myself, to understand the labour process in the manufacturing sector. We also followed up on cases of industrial accidents, union struggles, and so-called sites of labour unrest in the city. Some of these visits were with members of the People's Union for Democratic

Rights (PUDR). I found that even as the years went by and the urban elite in India prospered, the living and working conditions for the majority of workers did not change. I grappled with many questions. What explains the continued poverty of industrial workers? If this was the situation for workers in the most 'modern' sectors of the economy, what could be an alternative trajectory of development? The idea of *Labouring Lives* was taking shape in an embryonic form. My friends Aunohita Mojumdar and Vivek Chibber convinced me this venture had intellectual space and merit.

The actual writing of the book began in 2020 when the global pandemic took most of us by surprise and disrupted our set routines. The book would not have been written if it were not for Aunohita Mojumdar. She is the invisible co-author and silent partner in this enterprise – reading, writing, editing multiple drafts – handholding me, pushing me, and reining my impatience in equal measure – until the draft assumed a tangible shape. Ramaa Vasudevan, Ashok Prasad, and Vivek Chibber read through the initial version of the draft and gave very useful insights and suggestions. Budhaditya Das painstakingly and carefully read each chapter and provided extensive feedback. Steadfastly, he stayed with the draft till it went to the publisher and the press. Manika Bora accompanied me for a final interview with automobile workers.

I found my publisher in LeftWord Books after going through my share of challenges as a first-time author in the world of publishing. I am grateful to Joseph Mathai, Achin Vanaik, Nandini Sundar, and Harish Dhawan for helping me to navigate this process. Sudhanva Deshpande and Vijay Prashad of Leftword Books have been extraordinarily responsive and encouraging editors and publishers. I also thank Devi Vijay for meticulously reading the manuscript and sharing detailed editorial suggestions. My niece Anjali Aggarwal pursued her undergraduate degree in economics at Delhi University from 2018 to 2021. A conflict-of-interest rule of the university proved to be an unexpected gift. It exempted me from work related to examinations and gave me time to work on this manuscript. Naveen Siromoni designed the infographics used in this book.

I am deeply humbled and honoured that Professor Amit Bhaduri agreed to write a foreword for the book. For the longest time, I have drawn inspiration from his lifelong commitment to making a difference in the world of ideas and consistently challenging the limitations of conventional economics. My most profound debt, however, is owed to the hundreds of workers who welcomed me into their lives despite being overworked and underpaid. Their stoicism and their generosity have left a deep impact on me. I distinctly remember an incident when a labour union leader made arrangements for my interview despite losing his father the previous day. If this book helps you, the reader, to empathize with their lives and their struggles, it would be a worthwhile endeavour.

Introduction

In 2020, as a virus began to wreak havoc on our globalized and interconnected world, two sharply contrasting images became imprinted in our consciousness through television screens and social media. One was the haunting spectre of thousands of migrant labourers walking home to their villages, away from the cities and towns where the lockdowns left them without money, food, or shelter. The forced march home, with many dying on the way, revealed the stark reality of their lives – precarious in the extreme, their earnings so pitiful that few were able to save enough to survive more than a few days at best in the bustling metropolises whose industry relies on their labour. The other image was that of the opposite movement towards the country's capital, with thousands of defiant farmers across India moving towards the seat of the national government to demand a stop to the erosion of their means of livelihood. The farmers showed their staying power by camping on the outskirts of the capital for over a year, their needs met by a strong network of supplies arriving from the farms.

Around these two crises was a divisive debate over the kind of economic reforms needed by the country. In keeping with its policy prerogatives, the central government introduced new laws to bring about reforms in both the industrial and agricultural sectors during the pandemic. Both sets of reforms were touted to spur industry, generate employment, and better the living standards of the people. The introduction of the farm laws brought the farming community to its feet in protest, with reams of comments, analysis, and reportage in the media. On the other hand, the previously existing labour laws were replaced with new labour codes with little resistance and scant debate in the public domain.

This book seeks to meet a gap in the popular literature by closely examining the working and living conditions of labour – *the labouring lives*. As India competes with China and other nations for a share of global manufacturing, governments and business leaders focus on the need to make our labour 'more flexible' and our policies more friendly for business. It would seem that the global coronavirus pandemic has made many corporate employees and professionals more amenable to flexible terms of employment. However, this book argues that flexibility for industrial labourers is not akin to working from home or remote locations. Labour market flexibility alludes to the view that, like any other commodity, the price of labour – that is, wages and terms of contract – should also be determined by supply and demand conditions in the market. Yet, labour is *not just a commodity* – the life and living conditions cannot be left to the vagaries of the market.

This book combines first-hand accounts of labourers' lives with an examination of policy and law to illuminate the little-understood landscape of labouring lives. Based on interviews done over several years, the book provides glimpses of the lives of automobile and garment workers, most first-generation migrants making their way out of subsistence agriculture which is no longer enough for their survival.[1] By focusing on workers employed in the globally integrated industries of readymade garments and the automotive industry, the book seeks to shed light on what lives in the belly of manufacturing success stories really look like. Garments and automobiles also span the lower and higher ends of the globally integrated manufacturing industry, thus providing a view of the spectrum. This book takes the first steps towards offering insights into why farming families cling to their uneconomic landholdings despite the promise of 'rosier' futures in the industry. Examining the apparently thriving sectors also tells

---

[1] Unlike the garment sector, I have not reached out to the management of automobile companies for writing this book.

us why other migrant workers from less flourishing sectors – had no choice but to walk thousands of miles on foot.

Chapter *one* traces the structural transformation of India's economy since Independence. It looks at the transition of India from being primarily dependent on agriculture to the present. Did the manufacturing sector absorb the people who moved away from agriculture? To what extent and in what types of jobs?

Chapter *two* takes the reader on a journey to the landscape occupied by two important industries of the modern world – garments and automobiles – in one of the biggest clusters of these industries in Manesar and Gurgaon in the National Capital Region (NCR). It is a story of how a nondescript town and its neighbouring village in north India's agrarian plains became a global manufacturing hub and industrial capital. It is also a story of the world of work inside the garment and automobile factories.

Chapter *three* shines light on perhaps the most important thing that defines a 'wage-labourer', the wages they receive from their toil and how far these wages guarantee a decent life. Through the lived experience of the workers, the chapter shows how many trained artisans and skilled tailors in the garment industry are surviving on the edge of poverty. It also delves into workers' wages in the automobile companies, a sector that is far more celebrated in the media and generates much higher profits. Contrary to expectations, workers even in this sector are moving towards more precarious jobs and uncertain futures despite their role in increasing profits for their companies.

Chapter *four* explores the work conditions inside the factories and workshops. It humanizes the processes and mechanisms that deprives workers of their time, leisure, safety and the comfort of staying with their families. This happens routinely, and this happens incessantly.

Chapter *five* steps back to explore how the legislature and the governments have stepped in at differing points in history to offer some protection to the workers in the contestation between the employers and workers. It looks at why this blanket of protection began to erode over time, and labour markets were shaped as less rigid and more flexible. It also examines how a move towards 'flexibility' impacts labouring lives.

The concluding chapter or chapter *six* shows how the current path of industrialization is unlikely to bring out improvements in mass standards of living. How, then, can the standard of living be bettered for the vast majority? The chapter suggests answers to where and how we can go forward, but it requires a shift in the understanding that commodifies and dehumanizes workers and allows markets to be the sole determinant of employment, wages and work conditions.

The two *annexures* provide short analyses of issues and concepts thrown up in the chapters and some tables with data supporting the arguments of the book. The specialist reader may find them valuable. The names of the workers interviewed for this book have been changed to protect their identities.

1. Imagined Futures

Twenty-nine year-old Mohan from Mirzapur in eastern Uttar Pradesh is the first person in his family to have received a technical education, which his family hoped would automatically put him in a higher earning bracket than his father, who eked out a living as a mason. The education cost alone was an investment the family could afford only when Mohan worked for several years as an unskilled employee in a local hospital to save money right after high school. His training in an Industrial Training Institute (ITI) set up by the Department of Education qualified him for a job in a coveted sector of the manufacturing industry, and he was recruited on campus by a leading automobile company in 2015. Life seemed full of promise. Five years hence and after some tribulations, Mohan has a job he wants to hold on to as jobs are hard to come by. However, he is pretty sure he doesn't want his children to follow in his footsteps. Agriculture is no longer an option for the family, which owns only one bigha – less than half an acre of land- and Mohan doesn't know what opportunities he can steer his children towards. All he knows is that he doesn't want his children to go through what he does. 'There is no future in this line of work,' he told me when I met him in his sparse but clean room in Gurgaon, near Delhi.

Jairam Pandit, a tailor in a garment factory in Udyog Vihar, is considered by his colleagues to be one of the luckier ones. His experience and his tailoring skills have earned him a place in the sampling department which pays more than what ordinary tailors earn. But even after twenty years in the garment industry, the wage he is paid is far from enough. 'If we don't do overtime, we will not be able to stay in Delhi. We will have to run away. Anyone can earn up to 5,000 rupees in Bihar, what is the need to come to Delhi? If we don't do overtime, our earnings will be sufficient for only one person,' he said.

The first in their families to become industrial workers, Mohan and Jairam are employed at different ends of the spectrum of the manufacturing sector. Yet both seem equally without hope for the future. Jairam's investment of twenty years of labour and Mohan's investment in a costly education has not yielded the promised benefits. Young Mohan has lost hope early in life, while Jairam is exhausted and has given up hope for a better life. Theirs is not an unusual but a typical story of workers in India today. What happened to the dream of an industrial workforce that would lead people out of the desperate poverty of agricultural labour?

NEW COUNTRY, NEW HOPES

At the time of Indian Independence, industry was almost non-existent, and less than 1.5 per cent of workers were employed in registered factories. Industrialization had been dealt a deliberate blow by the British colonial empire, which was looking for markets for its industrial output and found a convenient outlet in its colonies. A grim measure of the devastation of Indian industry lies in the history of Indian textiles. During the 1700s, the British empire prevented India from exporting textiles while its economy industrialized. Ironically, some of the earliest labour laws in the Indian subcontinent in the late nineteenth century were put in place at the behest of British textiles manufacturers, who feared that newly instituted labour laws in Britain would give Indian manufacturers an unfair advantage of cheap labour. This, despite the fact that by 1800 Indian textiles were either banned or subject to high duties ranging from 30 to 80 per cent. Textile exports from Bengal – which had accounted for 25 per cent of the global textile trade in the 1700s – fell by 90 per cent. Half of the United Kingdom's exports came from cotton manufactures and virtually all of India's from its fields by the mid-nineteenth century. The colony had been reduced 'from the state of manufacturing to that of an agricultural country' as a director of the East India Company had predicted (Mukerjee 2010:50).

The reality of the lives of the majority of Indians emerging from three hundred years of colonial rule is captured in the iconic 1953 Bimal Roy film *Do Bigha Zameen*. The film opens with a sequence showing farmers waiting for rain on their parched lands. Released less than six years after India attained Independence, the film is a stark depiction of the lives of ordinary farmers at that time: dependent on erratic rain, and at the mercy of landlords. Many were desperately poor – a step away from impoverishment and two steps away from disaster. Roy's movie was one of several portraying the acute agrarian crisis when more than three-fourths of recently independent India depended on the land for a living, and agriculture constituted most of the country's output.

For the government of the newly liberated nation, industrialization was an urgent need. Until then, most of the economic success stories of countries were of the transformative power of industrialization. This was most vividly expressed through the textile mills of Britain and the automobile industry in the United States, both of which changed the economic and social landscape of the two countries. The traditional understanding of growth and development gave a lot of emphasis to manufacturing. From the late eighteenth to early twentieth centuries, cities grew, factories sprawled, and people's lives became regulated by the clock rather than the sun. Snaking railways, freight trains carrying precious minerals to newly built industries, large factories, running machines, buzzing industrial townships, and uniformed workers earning living wages have been the symbols of this economic and technological progress. Movement of labour from traditional activities in agriculture and other primary sectors to 'modern' industry was seen as the key to fostering economic growth.

Whether early developers such as England, or Germany,

or an even more recent one like South Korea, manufacturing growth has played an important role and for economists, this has been entrenched as an important goal in the global growth story. Manufacturing plays a special role in a country's structural transformation relative to other economic sectors, such as agriculture or services, as it is the one economic activity where there is a scope for raising productivity along with increasing wages. Unlike agriculture which depends on soil and climate conditions that are specific to each country and faces a limit to increase in productivity, productivity in manufacturing can be increased with the use of technology which is easily transportable across geographical boundaries. Manufacturing can create employment with its capacity to absorb people with a wide range of skills. For example, unskilled labour can be employed in low-tech industries such as garments where a range of menial tasks such as thread cutting and button stitching are required, or in factories producing basic metal utensils, where the skills required include stoking furnaces or hammering out shapes. On the other hand, industries such as automobile manufacturing needs workers with technical training to work with high-end machines and even robots.

Manufacturing's potential to absorb different skill gradations also means that the sector offers workers the opportunity of upward mobility, moving them, through the acquisition of skills, education, and savings, sometimes over generations, to a better station in life. In a globalized world, the fact that manufacturing is tradable works in its favour. A developing country is not limited by the availability of domestic raw materials or the existence of domestic markets. Inputs can be imported, and output exported. World markets can potentially provide near-limitless demand for manufactured exports from developing countries. However, manufacturing, which is dependent on foreign demand, would face the uncertainties and fluctuations of such demand.

In India, the question of developing industries creating employment and improving of material conditions of people's lives were seen as being organically linked and crucial for the creation of a new world no longer mired in misery, the uncertainty of weather, and gruelling poverty.

BUCKING THE TREND

However, the snapshot of India's growth path shows that its structural transformation has been atypical compared to transitions in Europe, North America, and even East Asia. In the case of the early developers, the route to development had two interrelated processes – the movement of workers away from agriculture towards manufacturing and services, and also the movement of workers from small-scale, unorganized and informal economic activities to larger and formal ones.

In India, people have been moving out of agriculture, but very slowly. At the time of India's independence, nearly three-fourths of our people depended on agriculture for a living. More than half of the country's output came from agriculture. Gradually, agriculture's share in India's output or Gross Domestic Product (GDP) declined, and by 2018-2019, agriculture contributed less than 15 per cent of India's output.[1] However, agriculture continues to employ nearly half of our workforce even today.[2] The mismatch between agriculture's contribution to India's output and overwhelming dependence on the sector for employment points to the fact that per capita incomes in agriculture are very low. Half of the country's workforce receives substantially less than a fifth of the country's income. The mismatch between the share of employment and share of output pertains not just to agriculture

---

[1] NAS shows the contribution of agriculture to be 14.6 per cent in 2018-19. Agriculture and Livestock together contributed 18.2 per cent of GDP in 2014-2015. The Economic Survey of 2020-21 shows this share as having risen to 19.9 per cent.

[2] See Annexure II, Table I for 'Share of agriculture, industry and services in output and employment'.

but is across the three economic sectors.[3] The secondary sector, sometimes called industry, includes manufacturing and non-manufacturing activities such as construction. The share of this sector in both output and employment has not increased substantially. It has contributed one-third to one-fourth of India's output and has absorbed around one-fourth of the workforce.[4] This is particularly true for manufacturing. The manufacturing sector's contribution to India's output has remained more or less stagnant, staying between 14-17 per cent approximately since the early 1980s.[5] In terms of employment, construction employs almost as many workers as the entire manufacturing sector, and employment in construction has increased 13 times during the past four decades (CSE 2018:62).

The major contributor to India's output is the service sector, with a share of over half of the GDP. India seems to have shifted from agriculture to services, leapfrogging manufacturing. It is sometimes argued that India can represent a different kind of structural transformation led by the service sector. While it is true that the service sector has led the output growth, it is equally true that compared to the manufacturing sector, the service sector has not created commensurate employment. The low job generation in the service sector is evident from the fact that despite contributing more than half of the national output, it employs only 25-30 per cent of the people.[6] There is also substance in the argument that the segments of the service sector which contribute majorly to

[3] Traditionally, the economic activities of an economy are divided into the primary sector, which largely comprises extractive activities such as agriculture; the secondary sector or industry, which has transformative activities and includes both manufacturing as well as construction; and the tertiary or the service sector.

[4] Annexure II gives tables showing the contribution of different sectors to India's GDP and to employment, respectively.

[5] The actual figures depend on the sources used. On account of changes in methodologies, it is difficult to find one consistent source for the contribution of different sectors to income and employment over the years. However, the tables given in Annexure II show the broad trends over different decades.

[6] See 'Possibility of service-led growth' in Annexure I.

national output provide employment to fewer people and require 'skills' such as software services (Aggarwal 2012). This means that despite India's distinctive role in the rapid growth of services, the sector as a whole is unlikely to provide a route out of poverty.[7]

A few trends stand out if we look at the three broad sectors together. The fall in agriculture's share in our income has been offset by the rise in the share of services in GDP. This has been particularly so since 2003-04. From 30 per cent of India's GDP in 1950, today, services contribute more than half of India's GDP.[7] Unlike in many countries, the people moving out of agriculture in India are not absorbed in the manufacturing and services sectors but in the construction segment of the secondary sector. Between 2004 and 2011, while the share of manufacturing in total employment increased marginally from 11.7 to 12.6 per cent and that of services from 23.4 to 26.8 per cent, the 'non-manufacturing' segment, which consists of construction and utilities, increased its share from 6.4 per cent to 11.7 per cent (CSE 2018:62). The service sector also absorbed some workers, but within the sector, majority of people found employment in lower end type of services such as petty retail trade, street vending, rickshaw pulling and e-commerce work. So why has India bucked the global trend?

LACKLUSTRE SHOW

The newly independent Indian state adopted the model of industrialization early on. The Industrial Policy Resolution of 1948 articulated the need for the responsibility of industrial development to be shared by the State and the private sectors. The first of the Five-Year Plans, which directed economic plans and goals, also adopted this. While the State played a prominent role in investment and regulation – a policy framework that has subsequently been criticized for its negative outcome on the private sector – the

---

[7] Depending on the data source, the figure may be just under half or more than half.

approach was based on the 1944 Bombay plan put together by leading Indian industrialists. The plan emphasized the need for a State-owned industrial sector that would provide a foundation for the fledgling industries. This phase was characterized by large public sector investments in key strategic areas and extensive State control over private sector activities through the licensing regime. India's Second Five Year Plan model emphasized building a capital goods sector.

From the 1980s onwards, India's economic development shifted from being State-led to being increasingly market-driven. The licensing requirements for private sector investments began to be liberalized and removed. With the 1991 structural adjustment programme, the Indian economy became increasingly open to foreign trade and investment. Many import restrictions were virtually removed by the early 2000s, and tariffs on most goods reduced drastically in the following years. The norms of foreign direct investment (FDI) were liberalized. From the economic measures of the 1990s to the more recent 'Make in India' programme launched in 2014, all governments have professed their commitment to expanding industrialization. Despite this, India's manufacturing sector remained small and did not contribute much to output or to employment. Manufacturing contributed 13.10 per cent of India's GDP in 2020.[8] To see this in perspective, the comparable figure was 26.18 per cent for China and 24.81 per cent for South Korea. Even Bangladesh – generally considered less industrialized, had a higher share of contribution from the manufacturing sector at 18.51 per cent.[9] So, what happened to Indian manufacturing?

There are numerous explanations for the small contribution of Indian manufacturing to output and employment. Economists broadly categorize these as supply-side – i.e., adversely impacting

---

[8] NAS gives this figure for 2019 as 18 per cent (Annexure II, Table IV).

[9] Read here for more: https://www.theglobaleconomy.com/rankings/Share_of_manufacturing/

the supply by the firms, and demand-side explanations, i.e., based on lack of demand for industrial goods.

The supply side explanations emphasize the lack of public spending, lack of infrastructure such as electricity, roads, ports, and low availability of bank credit, especially for the small-scale units. Subsidized credit is particularly useful for units in the small-scale industry such as garments.[10] Public investment in India has been declining sharply from the 1990s onward.[11] The withdrawal of the State from industrial development in India after the 1990s has implied a fall in public investment and the State's retreat from the sphere of industrial policy. This has been an important difference between the Indian and the East Asian industrialization experiences. As per the data compiled by the World Bank, investment rates in India had reached the levels achieved by China by 2007. However, the Chinese and the Indian rates began to diverge after that. By 2011, while Gross Capital Formation (or investment) as a proportion of GDP was 39.6 per cent for India, this rate had risen to 47.7 per cent for China. In the aftermath of the global financial crisis, while the State in China responded with massive investments in infrastructure and new technologies, the Indian economy suffered due to stagnation in both public and private corporate investments (Thomas 2019: 111).

On the demand side, demand for manufactures within the country has been constrained by low rural incomes and high-income inequalities. The majority of people lack the means to buy manufactured goods, whereas those with the means generate limited demand. International demand for Indian manufactures

---

[10] The shares of agriculture and industry in the total allocation of credit by scheduled commercial banks in India declined from the 1990s onwards. As a proportion of non-food gross bank credit, advances to SSIs fell from 15.1 per cent in 1990-91 to 6.5 per cent in 2005-06, 5.7 per cent in 2010-11, and only 4.9 per cent in 2017-18. With the crisis due to NPA and other problems affecting the banking sector, credit disbursed by the commercial banks to the industrial sector has declined sharply from 2014-15 onwards.

[11] Gross capital formation as a proportion of the country's GDP was 39.5 per cent in 2012-13 but declined to 33.5 per cent by 2016-17.

has been adversely impacted by the global recession. India's exports have slowed down with a decline in the global demand conditions.

During the planning phase, investment into capital and technology intensive sectors laid the foundations for India's diversified economic base, but at the same time, the employment generating potential of the capital goods sector was limited. Even later, the size of the manufacturing workforce relative to the country's total workforce remained steady at 10.6 per cent between 1983-84 and 1993-94, or only one in ten people got a job in the manufacturing sector. Most of these jobs were created in what is known as the unorganized sector and not in factories. Till the middle of the 2000s, factories failed to generate much employment.[12] However, after 2004-05 and till 2011-12, most of the employment was generated in the factory sector, but these were not jobs of 'good quality', that is well-paying and with job security. Post-2011-12, once again, the growth of output and employment in India's factory sector decelerated. After a brief revival, the slowdown has continued.[13]

Labour market flexibility

The 'jobless' growth phenomenon – stagnant growth of employment despite a relatively fast growth of value added – in India's factory sector between the 1980s and early 2000s has been the subject of scholarly debate. Some economists have argued that the slow growth of factory employment in India during the 1980s and in later decades has been mainly because of the country's labour market rigidity. However, there are enough grounds to contest the above assessment, particularly in the context of the

---

[12] The difference between factories and workshops; between organized and unorganized sectors is discussed briefly in Annexure I.

[13] A situation wherein the growth of an economy's manufacturing sector begins to slow down prematurely in its path towards development resulting in a shrinking proportion of manufacturing sector in both output and employment, is termed as 'premature deindustrialization' Annexure I contains a brief note on premature deindustrialization.

rising share of informal employment even within the formal segment of Indian manufacturing. Between 1999-2000 and 2014-15, directly employed workers accounted for only 33.5 per cent of the incremental employment in India's factory sector, while the rest were contract workers or other employees who are outside the purview of the labour laws.

Though employment generation was an early goal of investment in the manufacturing sector, this aim diminished in importance steadily. An important component of the 1991 economic measures was to bring about 'labour market flexibility'. Policymakers chose two related routes for this. First, 'Exit Policy' or changes in the law to allow easy retrenchment and closure, and second, replacement of permanent labour with contract labour. Various government documents and the World Bank documents in the subsequent years, emphasize that lack of 'flexibility' was a major obstacle in the growth of manufacturing. The World Bank document *Country Strategy for India*, 15 September 2004, stated this in the following terms:

> Restrictions on hiring and firing of workers by medium and large firms are one of the greatest challenges of doing business in India . . . Employment in India . . . registered firms (those with more than 100 employees) are highly protected. Any registered firm wishing to retrench labour can only do so with the permission of the state government, which is rarely granted. These provisions make labour rationalization in registered firms very difficult, discourage the hiring of labour in the organized sector, and are especially onerous for labour-intensive sectors. They are obviously especially burdensome for exporters who have to compete with producers in other exporting countries . . . .The Investment Climate Assessment 2002 found that the typical Indian firm reported having 17 per cent more workers than it desired and that the labour laws and regulations were the main reason it could not adjust to the

preferred level. Further, the use of contract labour is restricted to temporary activities by the existing Contract Labour Act (RUPE 2005: 72-73)

Current policies perpetuate this further dilution of protection for labour. Today the main stated objectives of the Government's industrial policy are increasing global competitiveness and enhancing productivity and employment. Along with the development of high-quality infrastructure and improving the conditions relating to 'ease of doing businesses', a significant component of the stated policy is the emphasis on removing the *perceived* constraints. High on the priority list of these constraints are laws relating to labour, that are sought to be amended to remove 'rigidities'. Department for Promotion of Industry and Internal Trade stated this in clear terms, 'Policy focus is on deregulating Indian industry; allowing freedom and flexibility to the industry in responding to market forces; and providing a policy regime that facilitates and fosters growth' (GoI: Ministry of Commerce and Industry). The Industrial Relations Code (IR Code) 2020 has made the government approvals for retrenching employees extremely flexible in establishments with less than 300 workers.

QUALITY OF JOBS

Along with the question of the number of new jobs, an equally important question can be asked regarding the quality of jobs being created for the workforce moving out of agriculture. Where did people go after leaving agriculture? Where did they find work? Did they find factory jobs, or did they work as coolies, vegetable vendors or as daily wage workers at construction sites? Did those entering the manufacturing sector find jobs with living wages or casual jobs at low wages?

Until 2005, most manufacturing employment growth occurred in the unorganized sector. Although organized sector employment did pick up after 2006, even today, most manufacturing sector workers remain in the unorganized sector (CSE 2018: 80). As far as the organized manufacturing sector is concerned, the period from1986 to 1996 displayed slow but positive employment growth. The next decade from 1996 to 2006 showed a decline in employment and was the worst period for organized manufacturing employment. Employment did grow after 2006, but the growth in employment 'pales in significance when compared to the rise in output in the same period . . . while employment roughly doubled in this period, output went up nearly 15 times' (CSE 2018: 69). Further, since the early 2000s, organized sector firms have been gradually replacing direct workers with those hired through third party contractors or 'contract workers'. The increase in contract workers has slowed since 2011, but a possible reason could be that 'contract workers are being replaced by newer types of precarious workers such as trainees and apprentices' (CSE 2018: 97).

The importance of manufacturing in creating 'gainful employment' cannot be overemphasized. Industry is supposed to unleash the potential of both individuals and the entire society. However, it is clear that job creation in manufacturing has not merely been inadequate but also of bad *quality*. Here too, the historical experience of development stands challenged. This becomes even more urgent given that a crucial route chosen for improving industrial performance is through making the conditions of employment increasingly 'informal' and flexible, making labour a disposable entity in many ways. While this path may create jobs, the jobs are increasingly more insecure. This is true even for the sectors that are globally integrated segments of Indian manufacturing, more coveted for providing better quality factory jobs.

Increasing Insecurity

Workers value job security. The public sector played a large role in the early phase of post-Independence industrialization.

Workers valued public sector blue collar jobs for the assurance of relatively good wages, better working conditions, and, most importantly, permanent employment. While private sector industry jobs were far less coveted, they too benefitted from the knock-on impact of public sector jobs. While the dismantling of the public sector annihilated hundreds of thousands of jobs, jobs in the more established industries in the private sector continued to provide secure tenure, benefits, and the promise of career advancement with workers assured of ending their working lives in a better economic situation than they started. Over time these benefits have eroded rapidly as calls for labour market flexibility led to the erosion of benefits and protections.

As jobs moved out of the regulated or organized sector to the unorganized sector, the proportion of jobs with the security of tenure decreased.[14] Permanent jobs gave way to contractual jobs for fixed periods of time, which in turn gave way to temporary employment on monthly wages and even more casual jobs at daily wages. The corollary to the arc was a loss of benefits such as provident fund, Employees' State Insurance (ESI) and paid leave. Increasingly, regular and permanent workers are being replaced by those with short-term contracts. Add to this, the loss of security with no assurance of paid work from one day to the next. Manufacturing sector jobs are becoming less and less attractive. While many like Mohan were forced to take those jobs as farming could no longer support them, others at the low end of the manufacturing spectrum continue to rely on agriculture to supplement their meagre incomes in manufacturing.

[14] CSE (SWI 2018) develops three broad categories of jobs indicating the degree of formality and informality. The broadest definition is simply 'regular worker' (Formal 1). The second definition (Formal 2) is regular work with the availability of one of the following social security benefits: provident fund or pension, gratuity, healthcare/maternity benefits, or paid leave. The third and strictest definition (Formal 3) is the above plus a written contract. In 2015, only 17 per cent of the wage workers were 'formally' employed according to the third and the strictest definition. A detailed note is given in Annexure I.

While the country has made significant progress in alleviating extreme poverty since Independence, it has clearly failed to enter the category of high-income nations. Much of the wealth generated is concentrated in the top one per cent, while mobility out of the minimum wage category has stagnated (Himanshu 2020). This worker vulnerability and precariousness came to the fore in the form of a humanitarian crisis of vast proportions during the Covid 19 related lockdown. The migrants included industrial workers who had no jobs, no savings, no food, and no means of surviving in cities employing them, cities where many had spent their entire lifetimes. Cities which they had built.

2. Locating Labouring Lives

The posh farmhouse walls in the Gurgaon-Kapashera area give no indication of what lies behind them. Euphemistically called 'farmhouses,' the high-walled private estates that run along Delhi's southern border with Haryana are lavish bungalows built on agricultural land and are a much-desired piece of real estate. 'You have the who's who of Delhi's elite living here, though honestly, I don't know who my neighbours are. All I see are tall gates and walls', says a resident interviewed by the business magazine *Forbes* in a 2014 article that identified Kapashera as a sought-after destination. The interviewee and most other farmhouse denizens are also unlikely to be aware of their neighbours who live in Kapashera's slum area, tucked out of view a few hundred metres away – the lakhs of migrant workers heading to the garment factories of Udyog Vihar in Gurgaon each day.

UNLIKELY CONNECT: AUTOMOBILES AND GARMENTS

The image of workers striding to the factory goes back several centuries. The textile mills of Lancashire in Britain in the late eighteenth century and Henry Ford's car plant in Michigan in the early twentieth century have become emblematic of modern industry. In many of Lancashire's towns, the mills were the focus of the daily lives of the population, who worked six days a week and up to fourteen hours a day. The mills soared over the slums, which housed the workers, mainly women and children. In the larger towns and cities, the mills' tall chimney stacks characterized the skyline for generations, testifying to the massive industrial output that transformed Britain into the world's first industrial nation. A century later, in 1914, Henry Ford introduced numerous changes at the Michigan plant of Ford Motors. These production methods brought in a wider set of changes that impacted the very structure of society and contributed to the United States (US) eventually becoming the world's economic leader of the world. The automobile industry created the 'modern industrial workforce'. In sharp contrast to the Lancashire mill workers, Ford's better-paid workers used the company's Model T car to commute to work, exemplifying the upward mobility possible for industrial workers.

The textile, garments and automobile industries also hold transformative potential for India. Textiles and garments contribute approximately 10 to 13 per cent of India's export earnings. India is among the world's top five producers of textiles and garments. Garments produced in India are exported primarily to European Union (EU), the US, and the Middle East. For the US, India ranks fifth after China, Vietnam, Bangladesh, and Indonesia in terms of imports of readymade garments. For the EU, India ranks sixth in its imports of readymade garments after China, Bangladesh, Turkey, Germany, and Italy. India is already an international player in the automobile sector and was the fourth largest manufacturer of cars in 2018.[1]

The two sectors, situated at opposite ends of the manufacturing spectrum, together provide an overview of Indian manufacturing. The automobile sector in India is of relatively recent origin, is capital intensive, and contributes almost half (49 per cent) of the GDP of the entire Indian manufacturing industry. In contrast, with its pre-colonial origins, the garment and textile industry is labour intensive and creates a third of the total jobs generated in the manufacturing sector (ET 2019). A 2020 government report states that the textile and apparel industry alone has the capability

---

[1] Source: https://www.ibef.org/industry/automobiles-presentation

of generating 70 jobs for an investment of every one crore rupees (USD 132,426) as compared to 12 jobs created on average in other industries (Nayyar et al. 2020: 05). The garment sector provides a reservoir for employment and its use of technology is quite rudimentary.

The automobile industry is based on a wide range of activities, from raw material extraction and processing to manufacturing automobile components and the actual assembly of automobiles. Automation in this sector has been very rapid. It has immense potential for transforming the economy and society because of its linkages with other sectors. Given that automobiles are overwhelmingly bought through loans, the automobile industry has links with the financial market as well. A technologically advanced industry employing 'skilled' workers at decent wages and jobs expected to improve living standards for large numbers is part of the imagination of the manufacturing sector and the aspiration of people joining it. An essential hub for this transformative industry is the NCR.

LAY OF THE LAND

'Gurgaon, a few miles south-east of Delhi, was one of the most backward tracts in the Punjab. A sandy famine-stricken area on the fringes of the Rajasthan desert' when Frank Lugard Brayne, the Anglo-Indian Deputy Commissioner of Gurgaon in the 1920s set out 'to transform the entire lifestyle of 700,000 people from their soiled cradles to their premature graves by making them industrious and thrifty'. – Clive Dewey

The British considered the 'Gurgaon experiment' highly successful, while Mahatma Gandhi deemed it a failure. In the early 1970s, Sanjay Gandhi turned to Gurgaon to realize his dream of the people's car, Maruti. Despite the dismal failure of that first attempt with its attendant political controversies, Maruti Suzuki

India Limited (MSIL) is today a core component of the NCR industrial hub, which has grown around the previously sleepy Haryana village of Gurgaon.

The NCR comprises the National Capital Territory (NCT) of Delhi, thirteen districts of Haryana, eight districts of Uttar Pradesh (UP), and two districts of Rajasthan. The 2011 Census recorded more than 46 million people living in NCR, making it one of the world's most populous urban regions. Manufacturing, especially large-scale manufacturing, is concentrated at the fringes of Delhi, overlapping with the states of Haryana (automobile, electronics, and textile and garments), UP (general manufacturing) and Rajasthan (marble, leather, and textile).[2] Gurgaon and Manesar are on the southern fringe, whereas Greater Noida lies to the east. The Gurgaon-Manesar-Dharuhera-Bawal-Tapukara-Neemrana industrial belt that stretches across Haryana and Rajasthan is an important part of the Delhi-Mumbai Industrial Corridor (DMIC). Launched in 2006, DMIC is part of an ambitious project of cross-country industrial corridors and one of the world's largest infrastructure projects.

The modern city of Delhi was built with post-partition and inter-state migrants, who found employment in the small-scale industry to eke out a living. However urban policy focused on letting the city space be used for political and administrative needs rather than for manufacturing. Further, orders for redevelopment of land on which slums existed as well as some Supreme Court decisions led to clearance of informal settlements. These slums used to feed the enterprises in the unorganized sector; consequently, slum

---

[2] NCR covers an area of 55,083 sq. km. It is one of the fastest growing regions nationally in terms of population and employment. There are 1,57,34,929 workers in NCR (2011), of which 26 per cent work in Haryana, 29 per cent in Uttar Pradesh, 11 per cent in Rajasthan and 34 per cent in Delhi regions. There are more than 50 industrial clusters in NCR, besides a number of micro-enterprises concentrations in NCT Delhi. The approximate numbers of people employed in the above-mentioned industrial concentrations are about a million with a total turnover of Rs 100,209.96 crores. (Economic Profile of NCR 2015; Report Submitted to NCR Planning Board).

clearance contributed to pushing manufacturing activities to the peripheries of the urban areas (Barnes 2018:141-143). Industrial estates like Okhla, which provided work to the initial refugees around the 1960s, gradually shifted larger-scale manufacturing to Faridabad district in Haryana, at the borders of NCT. This district had become the major centre for large-scale factory production and unorganized sector manufacturing by the 1970s. Today, especially after the economic measures of the 1980s and early 1990s, Gurgaon and Manesar have provided an impetus for rapid industrialization. They have transformed from semi-rural towns into NCR's main area of large-scale industry.

NCR is amongst the largest industrial regions in India, with Gurgaon and Manesar being important centres of manufacturing for both garments and automobiles. It accounts for about one-fourth of India's garment exports. It is one of the three dominant clusters of vehicle production in India. Together they make Gurgaon and its surroundings an important centre for export-oriented manufacturing. The area also boasts of other indicators of its globalized existence – call centres, offices of global financial institutions, and massive retail shopping malls. A visit to these malls, high rises, swanky offices and adjoining cafes provides no hint of the vast and sprawling world of industrial workers.

GLOBE TROTTING

One of the most globalized industries, garment production, has undergone multiple phases of geographical relocation. By the end of the 1960s, the more advanced countries saw a decline in textile and garment production. Subsequently, a network of exporting and importing countries emerged. East Asian countries, in particular, based their development plans on the Export Oriented Strategy of Industrialization (EOI). These countries exported readymade garments along with some other light manufacturing to further their national development, exploiting the advantage of lower wages. However, with a partial erosion of these wage differentials by the late 1970s, there was another round of geographical relocation of garment manufacturing. These included countries of Latin America, South East Asia, and China. Another process which accompanied this relocation was the spread of first-tier garment exporters outsourcing production to a second and newer or younger tier of exporting countries. India joined the 'modern' global garments industry only in the 1980s.

India has had a long and emotive history of the textile industry linked to the development of the Indian Ocean trade, colonization, and the anti-colonial struggle. The decade of 1920s had seen many significant struggles by Indian textile workers, not only against the mill owners but also against the colonial rulers. After Independence, the textile industry became linked to the efforts for the development of the entire economy. Some parts of the sector were reserved for small-scale industries to protect employment generation. As far as the contemporary phase is concerned, India's entry into the garment export market was built largely on the advantages of low wages. Through the 1980s, 1990s and 2000, only four countries had labour costs below India, i.e., Indonesia, Vietnam, Bangladesh, and Pakistan.

Both automobiles and garments have integrated India with the rest of the world. Our production has become part of what is called Global Production Networks (GPN) or Global Value Chains (GVC). Behind the economic jargon and the figures, what does this chain look like?

Journey of a shirt

If you enjoy shopping at one of Gurgaon's luxurious shopping malls, the shirt you may buy there is likely to have travelled the world before you actually picked it up from the counter. If you drove to this mall in your car, or even took a taxi cab, some of the nuts and bolts of that automobile may have been made within a small house in the slums of the NCR.

Consider the journey of a T-shirt bought from a Zara store in Delhi. The T-shirt is certain to have travelled more extensively than many people who purchase it. In 2017, BBC traced the global journey of a single Zara garment (Hope 2017). The material used to create it came from lyocell – a sustainable alternative to cotton. The trees used to make this fibre come mainly from Europe. These fibres were shipped to Egypt, where they were spun into yarn. This yarn was then sent to China, where it was woven into a fabric. This fabric was then sent to Spain, where it was dyed. The fabric was then shipped to Morocco to be cut into the various parts of the dress and then sewn together. After this, it was sent back to Spain, where it was packaged, and then sent to the UK, the US, or any of the 93 countries where Inditex-owned Zara has shops.

What is the journey of a Lacoste Polo T-shirt within India? Once the team of designers, usually located in the world's fashion capitals, finalizes the T-shirt design, the production process takes off in India. Lacoste's Bangalore office starts sourcing fabric from southern India. Lacoste's fabric is checked at the office and then travels to the NCR, Maharashtra, and Bangladesh for the stitching. The stitched T-shirt goes back to Bangalore for stitching the company's logo on the garment. After this stage, the T-shirt travels to Lacoste stores worldwide, ready to be sold. During its journey, the T-shirt has befriended machines from Taiwan and has acquired its logo from China. According to the 'Behind the Barcode' report by Christian Aid and Baptist World Aid Australia, only 16 per cent of the 87 biggest fashion brands publish a complete list of the factories where their clothes are sewn, and less than a fifth of brands know where all of their zips, buttons, thread, and fabric come from.

A typical situation is where a well-known brand such as Hennes & Mauritz (H&M) or Abercombie & Fitch (A&F) outsources production to units located in low-cost sites such as India. This order may or may not be mediated through overseas 'buying houses'. Brand companies or 'lead firms' act as global buyers and take the bulk of profits on account of R&D, design, or brand value. Firms in India, such as those in Gurgaon, produce primarily for exports to the brand companies. A garment produced in Udyog Vihar may have begun its journey as fabric in East Delhi's Gandhi Nagar market and is likely to be headed to a Zara store in Europe or a Gap store in the US. If one imagines a long chain through the globe, where value is being added at different links in the chain, Indian firms are located at the lower value segment of the chain. Since lead buyers such as A&F exercise commercial power and control through branding and marketing over suppliers in countries like India, apparel production is often described using the phrase 'buyer-driven value chain'.

Fast car, long drive

On the other hand, automobile production is part of the 'producer-driven commodity chain'. Before Independence, cars were assembled inside India. The import substitution policy followed after 1947 created a situation where only domestic manufacturers, such as Hindustan Motors, the manufacturer of the famous Ambassador car, existed. Only since the early 1980s did Original Equipment Manufacturers (OEMs) become entrenched in automobile manufacturing in India. OEMs are brands or companies like Maruti Suzuki and Mercedes Benz that assemble finished vehicles. Today, a large number of global OEMs and Tier-1 companies have set up operations in India. These include MNCs and domestic manufacturers. In OEM production, the process is more technology and capital intensive, and the OEMs exercise more direct control over component suppliers. They source their components from vendor companies that are usually 'tiered', a hierarchy of firms that outsource repeatedly. Part of the process could end in a tiny shack on a dingy crowded side street. Tier-1 firms sell components to OEMs, and Tier-2 firms sell primarily to Tier-1 and so on.

A typical situation could be where the car rolled out by Maruti is also dependent on a Tier 4 'company', which may comprise of only one self-employed worker operating in a tiny space with machines such as drills or lathes. The worker may be making generic parts based on the orders of a Tier 3 company, which in turn would supply to a Tier-2 company, and so on. OEMs such as MSIL claimed to have more than 300 key suppliers in 2014 (Barnes 2018: 45). Usually, the powerful OEMs drive the establishment of vendor companies. The vendor companies located at different levels or 'tiers' may supply to a number of OEMs within and outside the country. Since the OEMs outsource many steps in manufacturing to a network of component suppliers, the responsibility for production, speed, and quality is very often devolved to the vendor companies. The components are assembled inside the factories run by the OEMs. The vehicles are then rolled out and distributed through company showrooms or dealers spread worldwide. This journey is made possible by another kind of journey, one into the bowels of the factories where these automobiles are made.

JOURNEY TO THE FACTORY

Garments

They have come from Uttar Pradesh. They have come from Bihar. Some took the journey from Jharkhand, Uttarakhand, Haryana, Orissa, and West Bengal. Most of them come from families with small plots of land in the village. Others had been engaged in casual work or were self-employed. Some come from artisan families with a history of working with garments. But all of them have come to the big city to try their luck and make a better life for themselves and their children through skill and hard work. First-generation migrants, many have just arrived, while others have been in NCR for more than a decade, and some have spent their entire working lives here. A unique feature of the garment industry in NCR is the preponderance of male workers in an industry that women workers otherwise dominate. In a world of male machine operators, some women are employed for thread cutting or handwork. Of the workers who are married, a large majority have left their wives and children back home to save on the costs of living. The decision to migrate is rarely taken individually. Relatives or those known through village networks take collective decisions. Women workers usually come to the city with their family members. Irrespective of the lifetime spent in NCR, most workers do not have a voter card.

Once in the city, they are recruited directly by the garment enterprises or labour contractors. Many approach the firms through relatives and acquaintances. Factories put out advertisements and gate notices and spread the news about jobs through word of mouth. Many firms also use in-house contractors where supervisors, master-tailors, or accountants double up as contractors. External labour contractors are generally larger and supply labour to a number of enterprises. Some contractors may take up the work of an entire department inside a factory. It is fairly common for workers to move from one unit to the other, and the ones who have spent a long period in the industry have rarely been with one enterprise. The contract system in the garment industry is so complex that workers are often unaware of whether their employer is a contractor or the firm owner. The workers identify factories or garment units by the plot numbers of the land on which they exist.

I visited Kapashera multiple times over four to five years. Often, I sat outside one of the many small chai stalls on the busy Kapashera-Gurgaon Road to talk to the workers. Many of those working in the garment factories of Udyog Vihar in Gurgaon reside across the Kapashera border. Both sides of the dusty road of Kapashera are lined with *dhabas* (street-side food stalls), small mobile recharge kiosks, and a few fruit vendors in between. The Reebok showroom, one of the bigger shops on the road, serves as a landmark here. On other occasions, I negotiated the open drains and narrow mud paths to reach the workers' houses. In the slum that was once a village, I walked through the narrow by-lanes and alleys lined by small but tall buildings and tiny shops on either side. These buildings are homes to the workers; dark, cramped rooms, open drainage, four to five floored buildings with about fifteen to twenty rooms on each floor, two to three latrines per floor, and one washing area. In most buildings, my eyes took some time to adjust to the darkness inside the building; only then could I see small rooms all around. The rooms served as both 'bedroom' and 'kitchen' and were rented by either a group of workers or, in some cases, by an entire family. Generally, the rooms with families were more cramped with a bed and a table which acted as the kitchen slab, trunks for clothes and sometimes a refrigerator and a television. Sometimes, the clothes on the bed had to be moved aside to make space for me. In other rooms shared by workers, often kerosene stoves were used rather than gas, and there seemed to be fewer possessions.

Automobiles

Mukesh went to an ITI after high school and got a job in an OEM in Gurgaon through campus placements. Ram Meher heard of a job opportunity in Delhi from his social networks in the village. Both of them got hired by the same automobile company. It was only later that they realized that the 'company' that recruited them was also the same, a Labour Contractor firm, which provides workers to OEMs, and T-1 and T-2 companies. The majority of workers employed in these companies have been hired through the services of multiple labour contractors. Sometimes, contractor companies provide initial training to the workers about conducting themselves in the factories. When the companies need unskilled, casual workers at very short notice in crisis situations, contractors recruit workers from 'labour *chowks*'. These chowks are places by the roadside or under flyovers where daily wage workers congregate with their tools, waiting to be hired for the day.

The contractors range from entrepreneurial professionals with management degrees to ex-shop floor workers and supervisors. The commission charged by the contractor could range from 5-8 per cent of the workers' wages for the duration of the 'contract' (Barnes 2018: 161). The workers have varied job contracts - a small minority are permanent workers who can be on probation or trainees. Then there are 'company casuals' recruited for 2-5 years through the labour contractors, but the liability remains with the principal employer or the automobile company. In the case of 'contract workers', the automobile company has no liability towards the workers. Companies also take in 'casual workers', and trainees under 'National Employment Enhancement Mission (NEEM)' and as part of the skill enhancement programme under the 'Pradhan Mantri Kaushal Vikas Yojana (PMKVY)'.[3]

In contrast to OEMs, T-1 and T-2 companies, a job in T-3 can be landed by paying attention to the advertisements for 'helpers' or 'operators'. The lower-tier firms normally do not employ the services of labour contractors. T-4 workers may work alone or with family members and sometimes hire a small number of workers.

Automobile workers are often younger and unmarried compared to garment sector workers. They come fresh out of High School or ITI. Many OEMs have started setting up their own ITIs and giving certificates. This industry, too, has a preponderance of male workers. Before the major unrest in Maruti's Manesar plant in 2011-12, a large share of workers was from nearby villages of

---

[3] The NEEM and PMKVY are schemes to provide skills to the youth to enhance their employment opportunities. The objective of the NEEM is to offer on-the-job practical training to enhance the employability of a person either pursuing their graduation/diploma in any technical or non-technical stream or have discontinued studies of degree or diploma course to increase their employability. The Pradhan Mantri Kaushal Vikas Yojna by Technical Institutions (PMKVY-TI) is implemented through AICTE-approved colleges to impart engineering skills to drop-out students and find placement in suitable private sector jobs.

Haryana.[4] In response to the unrest, companies began bringing in workers from far-off states such as Bihar and even North Eastern states.[5] Upon arriving in Delhi, most contract workers find accommodation in villages around Industrial Model Township (IMT), Manesar, such as Aliyar, Khoh, or Binola. In contrast, better-paid permanent workers prefer to stay in cleaner but relatively more expensive areas such as Rajeev Nagar, Ashok Vihar, and Laxman Vihar near the Gurgaon Bus Stand, even though these are located nearly 30 km away from IMT, Manesar.

IMT Manesar, hosts some of the biggest automobile plants. Manesar is a world much more removed than what the geographical distance suggests. Tall boundary walls hide wide and clean tarred roads and large factories. Walking along these sanitized roads, I saw a handful of *chai-matthi* (tea-snacks) shops catering to the workers. The 'township' has one guesthouse for the managerial staff of various factories. Behind the guesthouse are the cobbled by-lanes of Aliyar village, lined by tiny, double-storey rooms which house the workers. The chawl-like houses are reminiscent of Kapashera. The rooms are pasted to each other chock-a-block with no sanitation or kitchen. The washing facility is shared, and voices carry across rooms, making it impossible to rest after work. The stench from a nearby drain is unbearable. This is home to many contract workers employed in the automobile plants. It seems like the surrounding villages woke up to the possibility of making quick rental incomes and hurriedly constructed matchbox-like rooms to accommodate the workers. Small and dingy rooms are on top of each other with virtually no ventilation and no drinking water. Every time the shift changes, hundreds of workers hurry towards or from their shifts in Maruti, uniformed and striding in

---

[4] Chapter 5 describes in detail the 2011-2012 labour struggle at Maruti, Manesar.

[5] In response to political pressures, the state government enacted the Haryana State Employment of Local Candidates Act, 2020 to provide 75 per cent employment to local candidates in industries. This has been stayed by Punjab and Haryana High Court and is under judicial review.

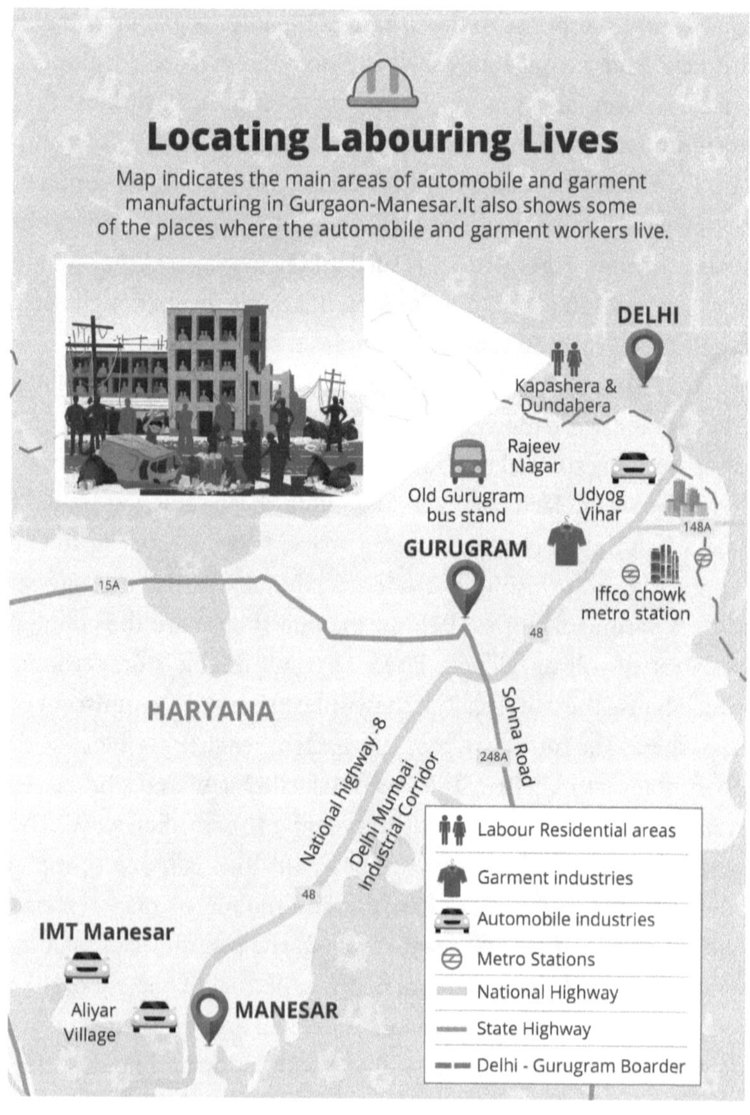

single files, each holding a two-litre water bottle; they look like the images of worker drones. I learnt the significance of water bottles eventually. The residential area does not have clean and safe drinking water, so the workers fill these bottles from the water dispenser in the factory and carry them back home.

Stitching together

The NCR specializes in the manufacturing of fashion garments. In the NCR region today, the garment units are primarily concentrated in Noida and in Udyog Vihar, Gurgaon. However, garment manufacturing in the region began much earlier, with the Okhla cluster emerging in the late 1950s. The Gurgaon and Noida clusters initially took shape as extensions of the Okhla clusters partially due to space shortage and rising land prices in Delhi. A majority of garment manufacturing firms in NCR officially fall under the categories of micro, small, and medium enterprises (MSMEs).[6] This official classification does not consider the fact that a 'small' company may register its multiple units as separate entities. The production in NCR is primarily directed toward exports. However, over time, some exporters are also tilting towards the domestic market. Some bigger firms may employ workers in thousands, whereas smaller units with merely ten workers also exist. Some firms subcontract part of the work to smaller units known as fabricators. These units take the orders from the main enterprises and get the production done. There could be further outsourcing as well. Registered factories and fabricators often give out work like embroidery, putting sequins on the fashion garments to home-based women workers in Delhi or even in further off cities like Bareilly in Uttar Pradesh. Many of these women are those whose husbands work in the garment

---

[6] MSME Enterprises

	Investment in plants and machinery, and Equipment (Rs crores)	Annual Turnover (Rs crores)
Micro	Maximum 1	Maximum 5
Small	Maximum 10	Maximum 50
Medium	Maximum 50	Maximum 250

Revised Classification w.e.f 1 July 2020 (msme.gov.in)

factories, and they treat this work as something which can be done in between household chores and brings in '*haathkharch*' (pocket money).[7]

World of work

Within the factories, workers usually refrained from talking to me, partly since they had no time but also because of the owners' watchful eyes. It was easier to meet the workers at their residence, so I made multiple visits to Kapashera, a village on the Delhi side of the Delhi-Gurgaon border. Kapashera and Dundahera in Delhi and Gurgaon, respectively, have a large number of garment workers. I also met some garment workers in Okhla and Noida. Meeting the factory owners was not easy, especially in the case of the larger units, but I did meet some in Okhla, Noida and Udyog Vihar.

The nature of work depends on the type of garment unit. Some of the larger units undertake multiple processes such as product design, marketing, making of samples, cutting, tailoring, embroidery, packing and shipping. Many of these processes are undertaken under the 'chain system' or an assembly line, introduced in the 1990s in garment manufacturing in NCR. Till the 1990s, 'full package tailors' prevailed. These were skilled tailors who tailored the entire or the 'full' garment. Under the chain system, each tailor is required to stitch only a part of the garment, such as the collar or sleeve, and thus has a lower requirement for skills. This makes most garment workers easily replaceable.

Once the international buyer companies have approved the design and the sample, fabric and trims are ordered, the fabric is sent for a 'wash care' test, and then it reaches the cutting department. The cut fabric carries its onward journey to the production department.

---

[7] According to the owner of one garment company in Noida, outsourcing by the bigger units was adversely affected by the Clean Clothes Campaign wherein the brand companies try to control the entire pyramid of production themselves.

This is where machine operators sit in rows, and the garment is stitched in parts, moving from one tailor to the other. In a medium-sized factory employing around 700 people, each row may consist of 20 machines and machine operators. A linesman is responsible for each row, and a supervisor is above the linesmen. A decade back, most garment manufacturers worked with cradle machines which operated manually. Today, button-operated computerized machines have replaced them. After going through the hands of multiple tailors or machine operators and needles of multiple machines, the fabric is finally turned into a garment. It may go off for handwork to home-based women workers. After the thread cutting and trimming, finally, it is ironed and folded by men and women bent over the finishing table. And then comes the time for the final destination, labelled, packed and put in boxes, the garment is ready to travel the world. Eventually, there may be cartons of different 'brands' rolling out of the same company.

In terms of hierarchy, apart from the managerial staff, merchandiser, and designers, the highest paid amongst the workers are supervisors, samplers, and master tailors. They are usually recruited via agents or labour contractors. Supervisors may also be chosen from amongst the workers, but their continuation in this position depends on their relations with the employers. Most workers are machine operators who often get into the job through the village and social networks. The few women employed directly are mainly confined to low-skill and low-wage jobs such as handwork, thread cutting or packaging. A large unit could produce for multiple buyers or a single buyer. Some factories also have a separate washing unit. Dyeing is usually outsourced due to the use of chemicals. Embellishment work on fashion garments such as putting sequins or hand embroidery (known as *adda*) is also generally outsourced. During peak demand seasons, even tailoring used to be outsourced, but in the recent past, buyers' compliance requirements have imposed restrictions on this outsourcing.

A smaller firm carries out fewer operations and is likely to be more specialized. Or else, multiple processes may take place in the same space. In one of the units in Okhla, cutting and tailoring took place in the same hall, which was the size of a large living room. There were ten workers, of whom three were women engaged in cutting the threads and making buttonholes. The past few years have also seen the mushrooming of 'training institutes' in Udyog Vihar. Sandwiched between multi-floored residential buildings and smaller workshops are single-room 'schools' with few tables, chairs and sewing machines. They 'train' people in operating the sewing machine so that they may find some job in the garment factory's chain system.

IN THE DRIVING SEAT: AUTOMOBILES

The major OEMs in this region are MSIL for passenger cars and Hero Moto Corp, and Honda Motorcycle and Scooter India (HMSI) in the two-wheeler segment. MSIL was the pioneer in the modernization of India's auto industry. It set up an assembly plant in Gurgaon in 1982 and another in Manesar in 2007. Hero MotoCorp has a facility in Gurgaon, and HMSI has one in IMT, Manesar.

The MSIL initially began as a joint venture between publicly-owned Maruti Udyog Limited (MUL) and Suzuki Motor Corporation (SMC) of Japan. SMC increased its equity stake in MUL and over time, MSIL became a subsidiary of the parent company. It launched the model Maruti 800, which soon became the face of an affordable car for upper-middle-class Indians. With liberalization in the early 1990s, the face of this industry changed. The Phased Manufacturing Program (PMP) policy was adopted to localize component production. MUL developed a strong base of vendor companies to have localized component suppliers. In 1994, the government de-licensed car production. Further policy reforms in 1997 allowed foreign firms to establish operations in India without necessarily entering into joint ventures with Indian companies. Also, companies were allowed to export components and ancillaries, and this furthered the integration of the Indian automobile sector with global production networks. As remarked earlier, today, MSIL operates with a whole range of suppliers belonging to different tiers. Tier-1 and Tier-2 companies are mostly in the organized sector. Whereas Gurgaon and Manesar have OEMs, Tier-1, Tier-2 suppliers, and some Tier-3 companies, the majority of Tier-3 and Tier-4 firms are in Faridabad and operate on a smaller scale. Some of those are workshops in the midst of slums. The Tier-3 and Tier-4 companies manufacture parts like spark plug sockets, ball joints or components used in engine production. These are then processed by Tier-1 and Tier-2 firms and eventually sold to the OEMs. Whereas OEMs, Tier-1 and Tier-2 companies are a mix of domestic and foreign ownership, Tier-3 and Tier-4 are largely domestic.

Inside the factory

What happens within the massive walls of automobile plants? The automobile sector has seen rapid automation, especially since 2014. Robots and workers work side-by-side – the speed of the machine sets the standard for speed of operations. A worker described the process of converting raw materials into components used in a car's door as follows:

> Every minute, 60 parts must be collected by the worker in coordination with the robotic arm and put through the machine to roll out the car components.

MSIL can also offer a glimpse of the inner workings of an automobile OEM. Press shop, weld shop, and assembly are the major processes in these plants. A few regular workers join with the contract workers in these processes. The gap in wages between the permanent/regular workers and the contract workers is not reflected in any difference in work. In some companies, contractual workers earn less than half of the wages earned by regular workers, yet their work remains the same. In fact, the permanent workers, 'company casuals', contract workers, and trainees work with each other on the same assembly line.

Within MSIL, the production process starts with the press shop, meant for cutting or pressing the sheet metal. Then there is the weld shop and the assembly line. From the weld shop, cars arrive at the sealer line, which has multiple workstations. Most of the workers at the line are temporary or casual workers and trainees. Bumpers are moulded, accessories attached, and the 'car' is ready to reach the assembly line. At this stage, different variants of the basic model are assembled. 'As a particular car variant rolls in, a light above the corresponding parts rack blinks with increasing urgency as the worker runs to it, grabs a part and pulls a cord to acknowledge he has chosen the right part. He then steps onto the conveyor belt, fits the part, and moves on to the next car' (Jha and Chakraborty 2012).

Conclusion

The tedious, repetitive, and continuous operation of the 'chain system' to roll out fashion garments or the urgent, automated assembly line of automobiles derives life and energy from the worker. Both systems force workers into a mechanized existence, their hands and feet working ceaselessly in a robotic, dehumanized manner.

Whether it is a 40-year-old artisan who had migrated to Delhi twenty years ago or a young 22-year-old ITI graduate 'placed' in the automobile sector, there is much more common to them than what meets the eye. Whether it is Udyog Vihar, the centre of garment manufacturing firms or Gurgaon Sector 18, the site of the first Maruti car plant or Manesar, which houses Maruti, other OEMs and some Tier 1 and Tier 2 companies, hundreds and thousands of workers can be seen walking or cycling between their rooms in multi-storeyed *chawl* like buildings in urban villages of Gurgaon and Delhi to their workplaces.

The automobile and the garment sectors together provide a window into the lives of industrial workers in a globally integrated world, and more specifically, they offer a glimpse of the conditions of labour employed in the manufacturing sector of India. The apparel and automobile industries illustrate the actual or the potential fruits of industrialization for those who are employed therein. They represent the two ends of globalized manufacturing, and jobs in these sectors represent relatively more coveted jobs in manufacturing sector. Did these jobs better the lives of a large part of our populace?

3. Indignity of Labour

It was the summer of 2014. I was on a bus with a group of young students headed to Kapashera, where we hoped to meet some apparel industry workers. We were going on a Sunday because it was a weekly holiday for most workers. Halfway through the journey (more than an hour from the starting point of the bus at ISBT, Kashmere Gate), we realized that some of our co-passengers were garment workers. I heard my young friends squealing in delight when they realized that these workers produced garments for Abercrombie & Fitch, a high-end casual wear brand. I was tutored about the details and nuances of this brand. Amongst those on the bus was Ramesh, a 35-year-old worker. He and the other workers were returning from Chor Bazaar (a well-known flea market in old Delhi). They had used their holiday to travel more than 30 km to the flea market to buy second-hand clothes for their children. The irony of the situation was not lost on us. Having spent their lives draping the world in some of the most famous brands, these workers could only afford old T-shirts worth Rs 35 for their children. Contrast this with the price of a flannel shirt from A&F, which retails for Rs 8,000 online in India.

I met Jairam Pandit, a garment worker from Bihar, whose job as a sampler got him higher wages than most of his colleagues. He told me, 'In the last twenty years, I have not bought a single shirt for myself. I always buy second-hand stuff from street vendors for 30-35 rupees. Sometimes I buy them for my children. We make expensive shirts but cannot afford to buy them ourselves.'

Why couldn't Ramesh, with a significant number of years working in the garment industry, afford new clothes for his children? Why couldn't Jairam Pandit? They hadn't expected to be able to shop at the glittering malls behind which they worked. However, why were new clothes simply out of reach for their families?

Wages are not only the means for meeting the essential and not-so-essential needs of the worker and his family but also the medium of rising and moving beyond the station of birth. Only adequate wages can ensure the same in a world where education and health must be bought. Can adequate wages or at least the minimum wages be quantified?

MINIMUM WAGES, LIVING WAGES AND FAIR WAGES

Ingrained in the vision of industrialization as a path to economic progress is the idea of a country moving beyond agricultural subsistence: of the bulk of its citizens benefitting from higher incomes and rising wages leading to social mobility. Of workers no longer tied to the vagaries of an unpredictable crop yield; instead enjoying the job security of a steady income and predictable work life. This is the promise not just of the higher-end of manufacturing, but even of sectors at the lower end of manufacturing, like garments. The garment industry's path demonstrates that journey. As country after country saw an increase in the living standards of its citizens, the garment industry's search for cheaper labour moved manufacturing to countries with lower standards of living. The logic of this course suggests that India, too, would have emerged initially as a source of cheap labour and increasing wages would, in turn, ensure a higher standard of living for its people. However, government policies have focused on keeping India competitive in the garment industry based on cheap exports. This was achieved primarily through reduced labour costs, mainly by maintaining low wages. But how low is too low, and how is this determined?

India passed the Minimum Wages Act in 1948 to ensure a minimum level of wage protection for workers. The spirit was carried forward from the resolution passed at the Geneva Convention of International Labour Conference of 1928. The resolution stated:

> If the labourers are to be secured the enjoyment of minimum wages and they are to be protected against exploitation by their employers, it is absolutely necessary that restraint should be imposed upon their freedom of contract and such restrictions cannot be in any sense be said to be unreasonable. On the other hand, the employers cannot be heard to complain if they are compelled to pay minimum wages to their labourers. Even though the labourers, on account of their poverty and helplessness, are willing to work on lesser wages.

The 1970 Minimum Wage Fixing Convention emphasized this, stating, 'Minimum wages, where they exist, should have the force of law and should not be subject to abatement; failure to pay minimum wages should be subject to penal or other sanctions.' The basis for determining minimum wages is as important as the concept itself. Are the currently determined minimum wages sufficient to meet the basic needs of the workers? Rent, food, travel, clothing, education, health, and maybe some leisure? How many of these *minimum* needs can be met with the wages received? There is little in the public domain about the costs of living for workers in the manufacturing sector. Most public literature is about the poverty line or helpful information on the cost of living geared towards the middle-class with salaried jobs. The information about industrial workers is made as invisible as the workers themselves.

Jagdish, from Bihar, is a 35-year-old regular worker at a reputed garment unit in Udyog Vihar. When I met him in 2018, he earned Rs 8,828 per month. With overtime, he earned up to Rs 13,000 to Rs 14,000 per month. Of this, he paid Rs 2,150 as rent for an 8 by 10 feet room which doubled up as a kitchen. The room is one of the ten rooms in a compound with shared toilets and a shared tap for washing. The landlord charged electricity at Rs 8 per unit, and the electricity bill averaged Rs 700-800 per month. Jagdish paid Rs 500 per month for water. He bought drinking water from the market. Since his immediate family – wife and infant child – stayed with him, he had no savings to send home to his parents in Bihar.

Ashok had a similar story to tell when I met him in 2013. Like Jagdish, he too comes back to a dank and cramped room in Kapashera after a long day's hard work. The landlord forced him and other tenants to buy groceries and daily necessities from his shop. Failure to do this would lead to eviction. Everything is more expensive in the landlord's store. For example, atta is Rs 22 per kg, whereas the market price is Rs 19 per kg. Ashok spent about Rs 1,400-1,500 every month on rations, and Rs 800 on rent and electricity. This is his share of the total expense for a room shared with two other workers. After skimping and scrounging, his monthly expenditures come to around Rs 3,000, including expenses like mobile phone. He saves Rs 3,000 from his salary, and the rest of the savings come from overtime work. Ashok's father owns 15-20 bigha (approximately 9-12 acres) of land in Bulandshahar, which he and his elder son cultivate. 'I cannot do agricultural work because I do not know how to do it. I was studying in school and did not do anything apart from studying. Education was of no use to me. Illiterate people manage to earn better than us. Vegetable vendors and *chole-kulche* (bengal gram curry with and bread) sellers earn more than us in a day.'

Responding to a survey conducted by the Society for Labour and Development in 2020, migrant garment workers in Kapashera reported having an average monthly salary of Rs 6,720. However, even for a tiny flat, the cheapest rental in Gurgaon costs around Rs 6,000 per month. The same survey reported that the monthly expenses of the workers were Rs 7,350, leaving many in debt or requiring support from agricultural work (Tiwari 2020). The idea of upliftment of the standards of living of the majority through manufacturing sector growth remains a pipedream. In reality, the manufacturing sector worker needs the support of the agricultural sector.

Can it be on account of workers' reckless spending? Alessandra Mezzadri and Ravi Srivastava published a survey report in 2015 of garment workers in the NCR, which details their expenditure on major items (p. 149). Food items (other than *paan* and alcohol) comprise 53 per cent of average household expenditures, followed by rents, which comprise 19.2 per cent. Surprisingly, education, although applicable to only a few households, takes up 12.8 per cent of average household expenditure. 8.5 per cent of total expenditure was on medical requirements and 7 per cent on transport. Low government spending on health and education means out-of-pocket expenditures on these essential services from wages. The survey concluded that more than three-quarters of the migrant workers (76.6 per cent) stated that they regard their native place as their primary residence. This reflects how workers lack a sense of economic and social security at their workplace.

Over the years, Supreme Court, through repeated judgements, reiterated the need for a legally enforceable minimum wage and has ruled that minimum wages should be determined by need-based criteria that extend beyond basic physical needs. Apart from minimum wages based on the needs of the workers, Committee on Fair Wages (1948) further introduced the concepts of fair wage and living wage based on the capacity of the employer to pay and the general economic conditions prevailing in a country.[1] Then, there is the National Floor Wage which acts as a floor for the minimum wages fixed by governments of different states. Unlike the minimum wages, no specific criteria are laid out to

---

[1] According to the Ministry of Labour and Employment, a tripartite committee, 'The Committee on Fair Wage', was set up in 1948 to provide guidelines for wage structures in the country. The report of this committee was a significant landmark in the history of the formulation of wage policy in India. Its recommendations set out the fundamental concepts of 'living wage', 'minimum wages', and 'fair wage', besides setting out guidelines for wage fixation. For details, see note in Annexure I.

determine this. Contrary to juridical efforts to expand the concept of minimum wage, the workers' reality has been that minimum wages do not cover the basic needs of food, clothing, and shelter, let alone education and medical expenses.

THREAD BY THREAD: GARMENTS

Minimum is the maximum

'The cost of living, including food and rent, comes to about 90 rupees daily. I have not gone to work today, so how can I eat? I will eat only twice today. I've had tea and breakfast in the morning and will have dinner in the evening. We eat twice on the days when we don't go to work; otherwise, we have food three times'. – Mubarak, a tailor employed in the garment unit in Kapashera

The minimum wage was meant to be just that, *minimum*. On the ground, this has become the *maximum* paid to most workers. It has become the ceiling rather than the floor. The very idea of minimum wages is that all 'essential' needs are met. In reality, the needs which can be met with wages have been steadily falling. When the wages are adjusted for the rise in prices, less and less can be purchased. Wages are considerably below what can be regarded as living wages.

Badaruddin Mohammad has worked as a tailor in garment manufacturing units for nearly two decades. He followed in his father's footsteps, who worked in a fabricating unit in Gobindpuri (near Okhla). When Badaruddin started work in the garment industry, there were fewer large factories, with piece-rate as the prevalent way of fixing workers' wages. The stitching rate back then was Rs 25 per shirt; on most days, he earned at least Rs 70 for his work. He came to Kapashera around 2003-04 to work as a sampler, starting with a monthly salary of Rs 2,100-2,200. In

2015, though his salary rose to Rs 8,000 per month plus overtime, Badaruddin felt his purchasing power had declined and he saved less than earlier.

The workers hardly, if ever, earn higher than the *minimum wage*. In 2019, the Haryana government stipulated the minimum wage for semi-skilled workers as Rs 9,268.75 and Rs 9,732.18 per month, for categories A and B, respectively where the categories depend on the years of experience. A typical worker in a garment factory, whom I met, received Rs 9,393 a month.[2] Workers in the unorganized units of the garment sector receive even lower wages. The Mezzadri-Srivastava survey showed that the mean daily wages in garment manufacturing for regular workers in the organized sector were Rs 221.11 per day in 2011-12 compared to Rs 145.18 in the unorganized sector. Some workers were paid less than the minimum wage. For the skilled category workers, the statutory minimum wages (in Rs per day) were 197 (Noida), 339 (Delhi) and 211 (Gurgaon), but the workers reported daily wages of 201, 263 and 211, respectively. This gap was greater for unskilled workers – the minimum wage in Rs per day was 156 (Noida), 279 (Delhi) and 191 (Gurgaon). In each of the three places, workers reported getting lesser than the minimum. Wages reported were Rs 140, Rs 247, and Rs 177 per day, respectively (Mezzadri and Srivastava 2015: 126).

Women in a man's world

Usha Devi had been working for five months as a chain worker in the production department for the Krishna label factory in Udyog Vihar when I met her in 2013. The factory was half an hour's walk from her home. She woke up at 5 am daily to complete her household chores before heading out. She made belts for trouser brands like Blackberrys. She faced a lot of pressure on the shop

---

[2] Every year, each state provides a list of minimum wages for different categories of workers. Annexure II gives the Minimum Wages in Haryana for 2019.

floor, stitching about 130-150 pieces of belts in an hour. Workers sat in four lines with 40 machines, and there was one supervisor for the entire floor. Each line was also supervized by the master tailor, who ensured that workers (primarily women) did not spend time talking to each other. If a worker was slow for some reason, she was sent home for the day. Usha earned about Rs 5,300 per month, which included Rs 700 for Provident Fund (PF) deduction. Before joining this company, like many women in the area, she had worked at home doing embroidery and finishing work. However, the middlemen who brought the work home from the factories extracted most of the earnings. Hence, she said, most women preferred working in the factories instead of working from home.

I also met Kiran in 2013. Kiran and her husband had moved to Delhi from Varanasi. She did the job of trimming garment threads at a garment unit in Sangam Vihar. Even after nearly five years in the garment industry, she earned Rs 5,200 monthly. The couple's earnings and some income from their land in Varanasi, enabled them to admit their children to a boarding school. After the Varanasi income dried up, they had no choice but to remove the children from the school. Kiran worked overtime almost every day and even on Sundays, primarily to provide a good education for her children. If production targets were not met at work, the managers immediately terminated the workers ('*Hisaab kar dete hain*'). Despite a 12-hour working day, she took care of all the domestic chores. Kiran talked about her various fears – the fear of losing her job any day, the fear of a husband who expected her to work 16-18 hours a day, and the fear of not being able to make a life with basic human dignity.

A small group of students and I met Sangeeta at her home in Kapashera. She was busy washing clothes in the common washing area that Sunday morning. She continued washing clothes while talking to us. We gathered around her on small floor stools. She and her husband had come to Delhi from Bihar. He worked as a driver. A rare woman tailor, she had worked in the industry for eight years and in the current firm for four years. Her monthly salary was Rs 5,800 with deductions of Rs 600-700 for the Public Provident Fund (PPF) and Rs 100 for ESI (Employees' State Insurance).

In the current company, working conditions seemed better, and she got an off on Sundays. She was remunerated at the legally stipulated double rate whenever she did overtime. At the end of the month, she had around Rs 6,000-7,000 in hand. In any case, her income was meant to supplement the husband's income. She told us about the sophisticated punching mechanism that registered their attendance. This job was an improvement over the earlier job. She quit her previous job during her pregnancy. The last company had a policy that if a pregnant worker chose to work till her eighth month, she would get the next three months off. But according to Sangeeta, this was a ploy to get rid of workers since it was practically impossible for a pregnant worker to do the stressful work in the 'export line' till the full term.

Rakesh, a trade unionist, works in a company where women are employed mainly for shearing threads. He said the company, owned by a globally celebrated fashion designer, does not employ women as tailors since they were required to work overtime and into late hours. The company did not want to take responsibility for the security measures this would entail. According to Rakesh, the company operated under three distinct names to evade tax payments.

Manju and her husband had migrated to Delhi from West Bengal sometime in 2005-2006. Even after staying in Delhi for 7-8 years, they had no proof of residence. She had left her children in her village since they could not afford the living costs in Delhi. She went to meet her children twice a year. When I met her, she only wanted to save enough money to return to her village.

Difficult as these women's jobs may seem, they are better off than some others. Women involved in packaging garments stand for several hours, even up to 10 hours, getting only a half-hour break. This results in a severe strain on the back and legs. They are penalized if they try to rest for a few minutes during work hours. Compared to them, the situation of women doing stitching is marginally better as they can at least sit and work.

Apart from the work conditions, women workers had several other grievances. They are not given maternity benefits, and pregnant women are often asked to leave due to the perceived decline in their productivity. As another worker told me, 'We are not allowed to get up from our seats without completing our target. We are told, "You can visit the toilet or take a break after completing the target, not before that." *Ro-ro ke kaam karna padta hai* (There is no option but to carry on working)'.

Women workers I spoke with said they did not face sexual harassment at work. Both men and women were paid the same for the same work, and there was no discrimination in this matter. But often, women were given low-paying work, thus limiting their earning capacity.

Piece by piece, day by day

The garment workers' wages are both at 'time-rate' or 'piece-rate'. The relatively skilled workers such as cutters, tailors, menders, embroiders, pressers, washers and the like are employed on both monthly wages and piece-rate wages. The monthly wages are based on an eight-hour working day. Workers may be employed at hourly or daily wages at a lower level of skill, such as thread-cutters, button stitchers, helpers and packers. Piece-rate wages are in accordance with the number of pieces the workers make during the day. Although piece-rate wages do not come with annual increments, some workers prefer it since it is easier for them to take leave to visit their families in their villages. The employment terms are so fluid that a worker who is employed at time-rate may later be employed at piece-rates.

Irrespective of the employment terms, no worker remains employed (or paid) for the entire year. While those working on daily or hourly wages and piece-rates may get work for a limited number of days per month, even those on regular monthly wages are laid off during the slack season, which can vary from two to three and a half months in a year. While the regular workers are re-employed after that, the slack period effectively brings down monthly average earnings by 15 to 25 per cent.

The introduction of new machines and a rise in worker productivity have not resulted in a wage increase. A garment worker in Udyog Vihar explained how the introduction of machines for most processes has only led to a decrease in the number of workers and has not translated into more wages for those employed. The machine introduced for making patterns now requires only one worker compared to three to four workers earlier. The use of machines for packaging has curtailed the opportunities for overtime.[3] The initiative to develop a skilled workforce has been subverted to push down wages further. As part of the Skill India initiative, some garment companies have taken in young men for three months at as little as Rs 3,000 per month.

Mahesh is a native of north Bihar. I met him during my visit to Kapashera in 2019. In his 30s, he lived with his wife and a few-month-old baby in one of the 17 asbestos-roofed rooms in a large compound. A large single bed, refrigerator and kitchen stove jostled for space in the small room. The only natural source of light and breeze was the door that opened into the compound. He was a 'regular' worker in a reputed garment export company in Gurgaon. He talked matter-of-factly about not finding work for 2-3 months in the year. However, he remarked that 2019 was experiencing an unusually long slack period on account of a slowdown in the business.

Workers are eligible for gratuity if they complete five continuous years with a single employer. However, workers reported that the employers encouraged them to terminate their current contract

---

[3]   An infographic in chapter 4 shows how the introduction of machines has reduced the number of workers required for different processes in garment production.

just before completing five years. The workers rejoin the same factory on a new contract within a week or so.

Fifty-year-old Iqbal Ansari has been in the garment business for at least twenty years. He came from the Gorakhpur district of Uttar Pradesh as a young man. His wife and three daughters stayed back in the village. In Delhi, he put his tailoring skills to use at a small Okhla factory. Iqbal relocated along with a large-scale shift of garment production to Udyog Vihar in Gurgaon. He found a job as a sampler in a garment factory. He was one of the rare people in the industry to get a written job contract with a few days of paid leave every year. Things could not have been better. Samplers or those who make samples are among the most privileged tailors in the garment industry. With two to four hours of overtime work daily, Ansari earned around Rs 10,000 per month. This was in 2013, and a contribution of Rs 175 towards the Provident Fund (PF) was deducted from his monthly salary. He thought this deduction was indicative of his 'permanent' status. The same year, he found a suitable match for his eldest daughter. He was confident his job would provide the ready cash for the wedding. After all, he could have borrowed from his PF. But this turned out to be false hope. He was not allowed a loan against his PF. After a good twenty-plus years of a 'permanent' job in the national capital, he was faced with a difficult choice – PF funds would be available only if he quit the job and withdrew the entire fund. Eventually, he quit his job.

Sampling tailors enjoy some degree of prestige in the garment factory. In 2007, the average monthly wage of these tailors in Udyog Vihar was Rs 3,900. This rose to Rs 7,800 in 2016. The year-on-year rise was lower than Rs 100 per month for some years. In terms of the buying capacity of these wages, there was actually a fall over these years. This is because prices rose faster than garment workers' wages. Based on their pay slips, we can see that the growth rate or Compound Annual Growth Rate (CAGR) of money wages was 8 per cent, and inflation was 8.55 per cent during this nine-year period. Since inflation was higher than the

YEAR	BASIC PAY (monthly) (Rupees) (Nominal terms)		RATE OF GROWTH (real wages)		PURCHASING POWER
2007	3900		2977.09		
2008	3976	↑	2819.85	↓	
2009	4304	↑	2741.4	↓	
2010	4739	↑	2708	↓	
2011	5031	↑	2634	↓	
2012	5400	↑	2583.7	↓	
2013	5600	↑	2413.7	↓	
2014	6030	↑	2451.2	↓	
2015	6200	↑	2371.8	↓	

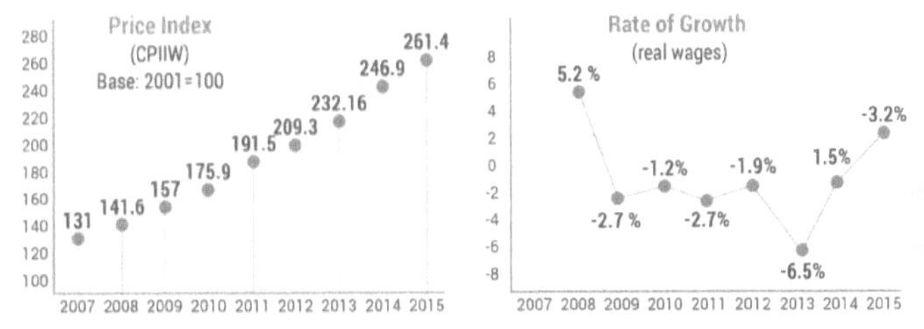

Salary/ Wages/ Earnings adjusted for price change is called real salary/ wage/ earnings. This has been calculated by deflating the pay in money terms by Consumer Price Index (CPI). Consumer Price Index for Industrial Workers or CPI (IW) is used with a base of 2001=100. Base 2001=100 means that prices if (of basket of goods normally purchased by industrial workers) in 2001 are treated as 100, then the index in subsequent years shows the change in prices relative to 2001. Hence an index of 131 in 2007 means that relative to 2001, these prices have risen by 31 per cent. The rise in CPI (IW) is the measure of inflation relevant for industrial workers.

Source for nominal wages: Interview of a garment worker employed as a sampler or a sampling tailor
Source for CPI (IW): Labour Bureau, Ministry of Labour and Employment, GOI

growth in money wages, real wages fell by 0.55 per cent (also see Table IX of Annexure II).

The high cost of low wages and reverse remittance

The wages are so low that many workers cannot afford to bring their families to live with them in the city. In the hope of bettering the lives of their families, workers spend a lifetime living apart from the same families. The work pressure, low wages, job precarity, and the high costs of living in NCR have meant that most workers rarely see their families, usually no more than once a year. For almost all workers, getting leave without jeopardizing the job or penalty in terms of slashed wages is a big concern. Many workers said they withdrew from their Provident Fund to visit their families. This was not possible for those employed through labour contractors. One only needs to imagine when and for what the salaried middle class is forced to withdraw their PF – certainly not to visit their family. A family member accompanied only 56.4 per cent of garment workers in the Mezzadri-Srivastava survey, and just over a fifth (22.5 per cent) were living with their spouses (p. 143).

Jairam Pandit, a sampler, has three children who stay with his wife in Patna. Every year during the winter months, he brings his family to stay with him for 1-1.5 months in Kapashera. For this, he spends about two months' salary and also incurs a debt. 'Only those families where both the husband and the wife work can afford to stay together in Delhi,' he told me.

Living apart from their families for long periods has become a way of life. In an ironic twist of fate, the job taken up for the family's betterment becomes the reason for living apart. This certainly cannot be 'normal' for human life and society. To meet the most basic of expenses, working 'overtime' for extra earnings is the norm rather than an exception. Another way is to compensate by supplementing the income by working in agriculture or having rations sent from the village.

Mohammad Ansari brought his family to live with him after many years in the industry. He is about 40 years old and hails from Gorakhpur, Uttar Pradesh. He works as a tailor in the sampling department in a garment factory. A skilled tailor, he came to Delhi in January 1990 and began working in a fabricating unit in the Gobindpuri area. After nearly seven years, he went to Bombay, where he continued work as a tailor. He came back to Delhi in 2004 and had been working here since. The family lived in a small eight by ten feet (approximately) room with no separate cooking space or windows. There was an asbestos sheet for the roof, and the compound had 17 such rooms. The compound was situated in a narrow alley in Kapashera lined on both sides with overflowing drains. Despite this, the salary was not enough to feed and clothe them. In 2015, his salary was Rs 8,800 per month, including EPF, ESI, and Travel Allowance (TA).[4] On average, he earned Rs 10,000 per month with overtime work. This was not sufficient to feed his family of seven. Therefore, they brought rations from their native village.

Many industrial workers still depend on agriculture to meet part of the family's expenditures. Many rely on multiple modes of livelihood. Packed trains leave Delhi during the agricultural harvest season, carrying the migrant workers back to their native villages every year. The city job clearly does not pay sufficiently to meet living needs. Most workers come back from the villages with sacks of grain to supplement their wages in Delhi. It is challenging to cover food expenses without support from their native villages and agriculture back home. Very few can afford rented accommodation in the city, and co-sharing rooms is the norm. While workers find it increasingly difficult to save enough to send money home, the high costs of living and declining wages have led to the phenomenon of 'reverse remittances' where the village economy subsidises the workers' living expenses. Most workers do not have a ration card despite having stayed in Delhi for several years, making them ineligible for subsidized food grains in Delhi. For most workers, the wife and children stay back in the

---

[4] EPF is Employees Provident Fund. The employee pays a certain part of the salary as EPF, which is matched by an equal contribution from the employer. ESI or Employees' State Insurance is a contributory fund with contributions from both the employee and the employer. It is a self-financed healthcare insurance fund. TA or Travelling Allowance is paid to cover the travel for work.

village, and their living expenses are primarily met through the village resources. The 'reverse remittances' from the agricultural sector are a 'second base of material provision in the city' for those who have migrated from the villages and maintained their rural connections. A portion of the worker household's consumption is met from the agrarian sector, whether as sustenance of a part of the family in the village or procuring rations for the migrant worker. This is how many can afford to stay in the city despite the low wages. Unable to acquire any permanent assets with their low incomes, garment workers are 'stuck on a circular treadmill between the village and the city' (RUPE 2018: 31).

GLEAMING MACHINES: AUTOMOBILES

In contrast to the garment sector, the automobile sector is viewed as the transformative industry of the modern age. The history of grimy, dark, dank conditions of early industrialization in Britain through textiles gives way to the white picket fence of the American dream, where the workers were also the consumers of automobiles they produced. Jobs in General Motors and Ford were coveted because of the guarantee of job security and upward economic and social mobility. While the glamour and social status associated with the American automobile industry may have declined, the sector is still seen as a transformative industry for the workers employed in it. The skillset required to join the automobile industry, including technical education, ensures that the starting point is a higher salary and better working conditions. In contrast to the lower end of the manufacturing sector, jobs in the automobile industry carry the promise of working in the organized sector, with tenure security, good wages, regular hours, and non-wage benefits such as Provident Fund, ESI, medical coverage and other insurance. The organized sector also offers the possibility of unionization, a body that will protect workers' rights and ensure they get the best possible deal.

This has been the case in India, where some of the best-paid workers in the manufacturing sector are the permanent workers employed with lead automobile companies or OEMs. Finding that first job is much easier for workers like Mohan, trained in the ITIs. Mohan was recruited on-campus by one of the leading automobile firms. So why does Mohan want his children to adopt a different path? As we shall see, the tiny sliver of good jobs is a sheer gloss over the mass.

Differential wages

In the spectrum of formal to informal jobs with an increasing degree of informality, permanent workers have better jobs. In recent years, the automobile industry has replaced 'regular' workers with short-term contracts. Permanent workers in the automobile industry are being replaced by contract workers, trainees of various kinds, apprentices, helpers, etc. There isn't much difference in their work, but the wages differ significantly.

The segmentation of the workforce based on contracts rather than the nature of work allows companies to pay less to workers who may be performing the same tasks as the permanent workers and, in fact, maybe putting in more hours and performing the more hazardous tasks. The wages and terms of work are also dependent on the tier or the level of the vendor companies, with the conditions in lower tier vendor companies being generally worse. The practice is to increase the wages/ benefits of a small proportion of regular workers and deflate the wages of the large majority of contractual workers.

The second largest two-wheeler maker in India is the Honda Motorcycle and Scooter India (HMSI). Based on interviews done in 2012, Tom Barnes showed that skilled regular workers at HMSI Manesar earned over Rs 29,000 per month. In contrast, the contract workers were paid a basic monthly wage of Rs 5,750-6,600 (without overtime). Of the 6,300 manufacturing workers at that time, 71 per cent were contract workers. Similarly, the Gurgaon plant of another OEM, Hero MotoCorp, had 80 per cent contract workers in early 2013. For T1 and T2 automobile firms in NCR, it was shown that the average ratio of contract workers' wages to regular workers' wages was 48 per cent for basic pay and 49 per cent for gross pay (Barnes 2018: 150, 156).

In one of the largest automobile OEMs, Maruti Suzuki India Limited (MSIL), the internal segmentation of the workforce is elaborate. By the mid-2000s, MSIL had moved a long way in recruiting new workers on short-term contracts through multiple labour contractors. These workers received around a quarter of the wages of regular workers. By 2007, the contract workers in the Gurgaon plant of MSIL were more than double of regular workers (Barnes 2018:112).[5] One of the three plants of MSIL in Manesar had only 10 per cent regular workers. Most workers, i.e., temporary workers, are generally excluded from pay hikes. In response to a protest by such workers, MSIL increased the wages of company temps in 2015 in both Gurgaon and Manesar. The new wages were Rs 15,000-16,000 per month (Barnes 2018:118).

In the aftermath of the labour dispute in 2011-2012, MSIL Manesar made changes that created a more segmented workforce. Since an important demand by workers had been the regularization of contract workers, the company started directly recruiting 'company casuals', 'temporary workers' or 'company temps' in place of contract workers. The company hires Temporary Workers (TWs) as fresh recruitments under the company payroll for seven months. After seven months, a fresh batch is recruited. Then there are TW-2, or workers who have experience as TW-1 and are called back by the company after a gap period. After the completion of TW-2, sometimes there is a test taken by the management, where some of the TW-2 are retained as Company Trainees (CT). A minuscule number of these may be 'regularized'.

MSIL recruited Ram as a TW1 worker during the campus

---

[5] 1,800 regular workers and 4,000 workers were hired through 20 different labour contractors.

placements at his ITI. After seven months as a TW1 worker, he realized that only '5 in a lakh' get absorbed as permanent workers. There was a *zameen-aasmaan ka antar* (huge gap) between what was promised and the actual situation.

In yet another process, diploma-holders or B.Tech degree holders are taken in as 'trainees' for one to three years, under categories such as 'Diploma Trainee (DT)', 'Diploma Apprentice', 'Engineering Trainee', 'Diploma Engineering Trainee' etc. More recently, 'student trainees' have been recruited under mission NEEM. They are hired for a period of three months to three years to work and study, after which they are given a certificate. Not considered 'workers', they are paid a 'stipend' equivalent to minimum wages. They are subject to a code of conduct under the Apprentice Act and can be thrown out (and certificate withheld) if they are perceived to have misbehaved. Then there are trainees under PMKVY. They are not paid anything or provided with any food in the canteen. All they receive is a 'dress' and a certificate at the end of the 'training'.

Significant wage increases for permanent workers have accompanied this shift in labour relations. This gets reflected in the differential wages received by different categories of workers. In the Maruti Suzuki Gurgaon plant, the starting monthly wage of a permanent worker was Rs 40,000-45,000 in January 2018, whereas TW1, TW2 as well as CT received Rs 19,800 in hand. Contract workers received Rs 17,000, and ST received Rs 10,400. Apprentices received Rs 13,500.[6] Workers receiving differential wages work on

---

[6] Wages for different categories of workers

Category	Permanent	TW1	TW2	CT	ST	Apprentice	Contract
Monthly Salary (Rs) (January 2018)	40-45,000 (starting)	19,800 (in hand)	19,800 (in hand)	19,800 (in hand)	10,400	13,500	17,000

Source: Amit and Nayanjyoti 2018: 26.

the same assembly line with virtually no difference in the nature of work. MSIL Gurgaon's vehicle inspection department has a total of 90 workers, of which only 10-15 are permanent workers. There are around 10 student trainees; the rest are temporary and contract workers (Amit and Nayanjyoti 2018: 26).

MSIL is merely a case in point. Tier 1 and Tier 2 companies started emulating the practices of MSIL. In the automobile sector, company after company, OEMs and vendor companies have been recruiting new workers on temporary and short-term contracts for a wage significantly lower than that of the regular workers. The proportion of regular and 'temporary' workers may be more skewed in the case of vendor companies. In 2009, the proportion of regular workers at Sunbeam Auto, a component manufacturer, was less than one-fifth of the total workers (Barnes 2018: 129). The Industrial Relations Code, 2020 provides a legal framework for ushering in the concept of 'fixed-term employment', even in the case of jobs of a permanent nature.

Under the knife

Segmentation makes it easier to retrench the workers. Internal segmentation acts as a deterrent to worker solidarity. Categories like apprentices or trainees are not considered as workers. The temporary or contractual workers can be laid off more easily during crises. This becomes easier when the company does not recruit directly but through labour contractors. Honda Motorcycle and Scooter India (HMSI), the second largest two-wheeler maker in India, was in the news in 2019 over the retrenchment of contract workers on account of a 'slowdown'. According to The Economic Times, the standoff at the facility, which employs around 1,900 permanent workers and 2,500 contract workers, began on the morning of 5 November when the company management did not allow some contractual workers to go inside the plant.[7] A

---

[7] Source: https://economictimes.indiatimes.com/industry/auto/auto-news/h msis-manesar-plant-workers-protest-against-sacking-of-contractual-staff/

prolonged agitation ensued over the next four months, which ended on 4 March 2020 after a 'settlement' between contracting agencies and the 2,458 protesting contract workers. Interestingly the company was nowhere in the picture (Chhabra 2020). Some contract workers had worked in the company for over a decade. A stylised illustration of HMSI contract worker's wage slip (see overleaf) shows that the basic pay after having worked 30 days of the month was Rs 9,500. After adding various allowances, it added up to Rs 16,200.

Segmentation between different worker categories occurs not just in the workplace but also on the payslip. The wage contract is sometimes specified in a way where part of the wages is linked to productivity or attendance. This makes it easier to pay lower wages on the grounds of 'unsatisfactory' performance. This effectively penalises absence and ensures that workers do not take (or are not allowed to) take any day off.

Mahesh, an ITI graduate, worked as a contract worker at HMSI for 10 years. Till 2019, he used to earn Rs 14,000 per month. Beyond the scheduled off on Sunday, an absence of one day cost him Rs 666. He rued that in once when he took three days of unanticipated leave, nearly Rs 4,000 were deducted from his salary. (The deduction included the production allowance for the entire month, i.e., Rs 1,250.)

In the Maruti-Suzuki Manesar plant, 'to ensure workers' participation, their incentives were aligned to production' (Jha and Chakraborty 2012: 12). According to the workers, SPM Autocomp Private Limited in Manesar has a policy of giving an attendance bonus to those workers who are present for 26 days in a month (entire month excluding one off day per week). Till 2017, no worker had received this bonus.

During times of crisis or lower profits, the OEMs pressurize the component suppliers to reduce costs. The component suppliers

articleshow/72263279.cms?from=mdr

pass on this burden to their workers. Thus, for most automobile workers with differing kinds of 'temporary' contracts, wages are not very different from the minimum wage in the industry.

Living wages and fair wages

Mohan has been employed as a contract worker in an automobile company in Manesar since 2015. I visited him in the early months of 2021. He informed me that his gross monthly wage began at Rs 8,800, was raised to Rs 11,000 and just two months previously, had become Rs 13,000. Mohan achieved this salary after five years of work. The wages sound considerably higher than that of the garment workers. But why Mohan doesn't feel he has made it good is quite understandable when one looks at the costs of living he incurs. Of the Rs 11,000, deductions were made for PF, canteen facility (Rs 300 for tea, snacks and lunch) and ESI. Initially, he had taken up a room with other workers in Aliyar village in Manesar itself. The rent there was Rs 3,500, which the three of them shared. But Mohan could not adjust there. The rooms were pasted to each other chock-a-block with no sanitation or kitchen. They shared the washing facility. Voices carried across rooms, making it impossible to rest after work. Further, the stench from a nearby drain was unbearable.

Mohan moved to a room in Rajiv Nagar. He now pays Rs 5,000 as rent for sharing the room with another worker from his own village. He pays Rs 500 on the conveyance for the company bus, since his accommodation is now 50 minutes to an hour from the company. The landlady stays on the ground floor and has rented out the two rooms on the first floor. Each room has a separate kitchen, but the washroom is shared. The alley leading to the room is cobbled. Clean, marble stairs lead upstairs. The small eight by eight feet room has been kept very neatly. It comprises a double bed, an almirah provided by the landlady, a small table and a rack in a wall for odd things. Although he pays more for rent and conveyance, he feels much better in the present room due to

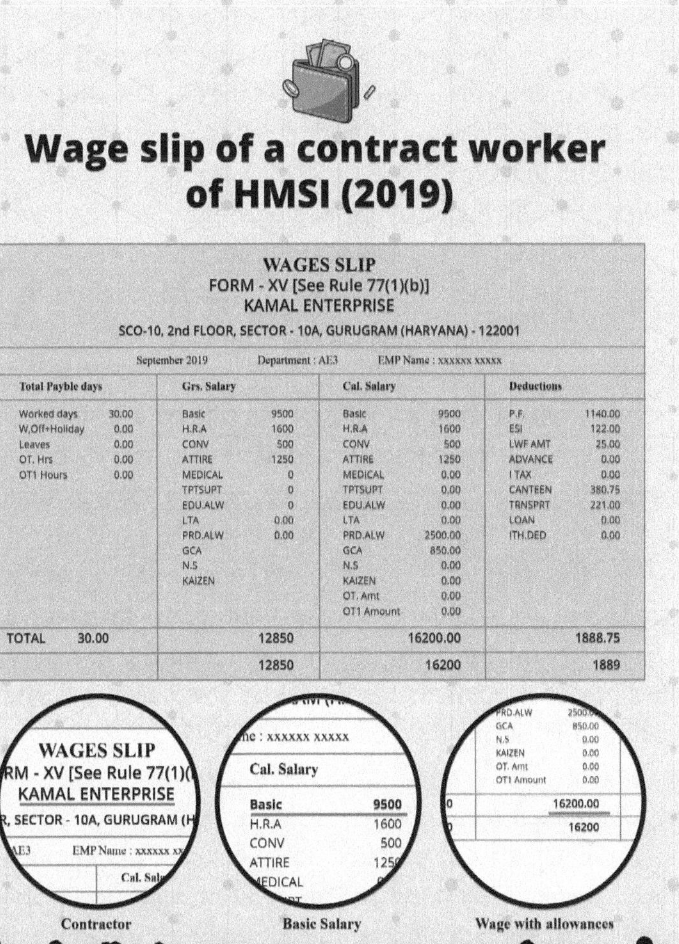

Wage slip of a contract worker of HMSI (2019)

WAGES SLIP
FORM - XV [See Rule 77(1)(b)]
KAMAL ENTERPRISE

SCO-10, 2nd FLOOR, SECTOR - 10A, GURUGRAM (HARYANA) - 122001

September 2019   Department : AE3   EMP Name : xxxxxx xxxxx

Total Payble days		Grs. Salary		Cal. Salary		Deductions	
Worked days	30.00	Basic	9500	Basic	9500	P.F.	1140.00
W,Off+Holiday	0.00	H.R.A	1600	H.R.A	1600	ESI	122.00
Leaves	0.00	CONV	500	CONV	500	LWF AMT	25.00
OT. Hrs	0.00	ATTIRE	1250	ATTIRE	1250	ADVANCE	0.00
OT1 Hours	0.00	MEDICAL	0	MEDICAL	0.00	I TAX	0.00
		TPTSUPT	0	TPTSUPT	0.00	CANTEEN	380.75
		EDU.ALW	0	EDU.ALW	0.00	TRNSPRT	221.00
		LTA	0.00	LTA	0.00	LOAN	0.00
		PRD.ALW	0.00	PRD.ALW	2500.00	ITH.DED	0.00
		GCA		GCA	850.00		
		N.S		N.S	0.00		
		KAIZEN		KAIZEN	0.00		
				OT. Amt	0.00		
				OT1 Amount	0.00		
TOTAL	30.00		12850		16200.00		1888.75
			12850		16200		1889

Contractor   Basic Salary   Wage with allowances

hygiene and cleanliness. A sense of pride in maintaining his sparse living space was evident when I met him.

I met Mohan on a Sunday, and he had come back from the 'C shift' (night shift) a few hours back. He had washed his clothes and cleaned the room. The bed had a faded but clean bedsheet. A Prestige water kettle sat proudly on the table. He served me warm water from the kettle, bakery biscuits, and a dry mixture. Mohan told me that he does not save anything after paying for rent, food, and conveyance. This is also because of the frequent trips he needs to make to his village since his mother has cancer. Each trip costs a minimum of Rs 1,000.

Additionally, his wages are deducted if he needs to take leave beyond the entitled seven leaves for a year. Mohan is getting his mother treated in an ESI-designated hospital back home. He says that they could not have afforded his mother's treatment without the ESI card.

A large majority of automobile workers are not able to better their lives in any significant manner. They spend long years working at low wages, hoping to become permanent someday. More often than not, the hope turns out to be a mirage. For the country, the automobile industry saw considerable growth in the decade 2000-01 to 2009-10. Workers did receive increased wages in rupee terms. But after discounting for inflation, real wages, which show the purchasing power of the wages, actually 'fell continuously' during this period (RUPE 2012: 5).

Overtime is the norm

Garments or automobiles, long hours are commonplace. History seems to have turned on its head, and the situation in many industries is reminiscent of the eighteenth century. Ford's eight-hour working day is a thing of the past. This is especially true for vendor companies and component suppliers. Like garments, the double rate for Overtime (OT) remains an exception.

In some cases, OT was remunerated at less than single rate. A case in point is a vendor company in Manesar which paid OT to the helpers at less than single rate.[8] A vendor company in Faridabad

---

[8] JV Auto is situated on Plot 113, Sector 3, IMT, Manesar. The company manufactures components for Maruti. Out of 150 workers, only 14-15 are permanent. The wages of the helpers and machine operators is Rs 4,214. The overtime pay for the helpers is less than the single rate, Rs 17.50 per hour (Jha and Chakraborty 2012: 28).

provided Rs 25 for food when the working hours exceeded twelve hours (Jha and Chakraborty 2012: 28-29). The pervasiveness of OT can be seen sharply in the ensuing chapter.

Are falling real wages, worker segmentation, and salary segmentation necessary, given the state of the automobile industry? Are workers paying the cost of diminishing productivity? Quite the contrary. Data shows that productivity in the manufacturing sector has increased. Between 1982 and 2015, labour productivity increased six times as measured by real gross value added per employee.

The rise in productivity has not translated into higher wages in real terms or increased leisure time for the workers. This means that neither are the workers adequately compensated for their contribution to output, nor are they earning *fair wages*. The share of wages in the total value addition of the automobile industry has witnessed a sharp fall. In 2000-01 workers' wages were 27.4 per cent of value added. By 2009-10, the ratio had fallen to 15. 4 per cent (RUPE 2012: 6). For the country as a whole, wage growth, particularly in the organized manufacturing sector, has been dwarfed by a much larger increase in labour productivity, with a resulting collapse in the labour share of income in this sector. On average, productivity grew at 5.5 per cent per year in real terms, while the real wage rate grew at 1.4 per cent per year (SWI 2018: 113). This gap between wages and productivity is also seen in the unorganized manufacturing sector (SWI 2018: 115).

So, where are the wages headed now?

The new labour codes include a separate code on wages (discussed in detail in Annexure I). The Code on Wages, 2019, states that state governments cannot declare a minimum wage *below* the national floor wage declared by the Central government at the national level. Unlike the minimum wage, no specific criteria are laid out to determine the floor wage. This is likely to adversely impact the minimum wages set by different states since they are supposed to take the national floor wage as the *floor*. This would be particularly so in a world where each state desires to be more competitive than the other to attract foreign capital.

Another labour code, Social Security Code 2020, states that a company can exit the ESI scheme if the owners and majority of workers decide to do so. For Mohan, this will mean that he may not be able to afford medical treatment for his mother. Annexure I describes in detail other provisions of the Social Security Code that will further weaken the wage security of industrial workers.

Conclusion

Why do people work? The obvious answer to the seemingly banal question in the context of workers is to earn a wage – a decent wage which can uplift the standards of living for the workers and their families. The garment workers' wages are close to the poverty levels. The Economic Survey of Delhi for 2019-2020 states that the per capita monthly urban poverty line in Delhi was Rs 1,134 in 2011-12 (GNCTD 2021: Chapter 20). This turns out to be Rs 5,670 for a family of five members. Usha Devi received Rs 5,300 per month in 2013 or two years after 2011-12. Kishan earned Rs 5,700 per month if he did not do overtime. If a worker is the family's sole earning member and there is no support from the village, the wages in the garment sector can just about sustain the worker's family at poverty levels. This is despite being employed and working hard.

Keeping wages and production costs low is an essential consideration for the owners of garment factories. But how low is it really necessary to keep the labour costs? A Lacoste polo T-shirt which sells for around Rs 4,000 in the retail market, is unlikely to have more than Rs 100-150 as wage cost. According to the representative of a garment manufacturing firm, a rough break up would be Rs 700 for the fabric, Rs 30 for stitching, Rs 10 for thread cutting, Rs 60-70 for packing, and around Rs 10 as the margin of the firm in NCR undertaking the stitching, and Rs 500 for finishing and putting the logo. The brand company milks the bulk of profits ranging from 60-65 per cent. The bigger the brand, the greater the margin.

Workers in the automobile industry certainly enjoy higher wages and are not poor. Indeed, they may be among the highest-paid workers in the manufacturing sector. Yet it is only a rapidly falling minority of permanent workers who receive decent wages. An increasing majority of workers, both in the OEMs and the vendor companies, have short-term work contracts and earn a little over the minimum wages.

In the automobile sector, the gap between the wages and the efforts put in by the workers has been growing. Technological advancement has been accompanied by better wages for a minuscule of workers but a wage deflation for the majority. Of course, the wages are not low for those employed in the automobile sector. A recent report on the pay ratios of India's top executives revealed that Jindal Steel Works CEO earned 1,052 times more than the average staff. The report added that the Chief Executive Officer of Hero Motocorp was the highest paid in 2019-20, with a salary of Rs 85 crore. Hero Motocorp reported the highest pay ratio for 2019-20, with the CEO earning 752 times more than the average worker. The lowest pay ratio was recorded at Maruti Suzuki. The CEO earned 39 times more than the company's employees (Khera and Yadav 2020).

While poverty is a question of *absolute* levels and insufficient material resources for a decent life, inequality is a question of *relative* distribution and the aspirations that remain unfulfilled even while working in a high-wage industry. International Labour Organisation's (ILO) agenda for 2030 includes 'decent work'. Decent work sums up the aspirations of people in their working lives. Apart from a fair income, it also includes a dignified work environment, security in the workplace and social protection for the families.

4. Stop Clocks and Unending Days: The Real Costs of Cost-Cutting on Worker's Lives

A visit in the summer of 2014. Along with a group of students and research scholars, I went to a unit in NCR engaged in manufacturing leather garments for exports. The company's management obliged around 15 of us by taking us around the unit. After seeing the 'pattern making' and 'cutting', we went to a large hall with nearly three columns and twenty rows of desks and chairs. Each desk had a sewing machine with a tailor seated behind it. We walked into a hall with nearly 60 tailors, but the only sound was the noisy whirring of the sewing machines. We could see the back of the tailors bent over their work intently. As our group walked in, some of the men turned around to look at us. Even so, it seemed like their feet did not stop pedalling, and their fingers remained taut on the garment. Some of them may have stopped for a few seconds. We returned to the conference room after the tour of the factory. In the subsequent discussion with the owners, we were told that the act of the workers turning around to see us was a 'wastage of time'; the few seconds spent idle were 'idle machine time'.

Time seems caught in a double warp in the NCR's industrial belt. Udyog Vihar's garment factories almost seem anachronistic: workers at tables arranged in long rows, hunched over pedal-operated sewing machines, the soft whirr and clack of pieces of cloth transformed into garments destined for malls in a global market, their lives not significantly different from that of their forefathers. Underpaid, living just above the subsistence level, they return each day to dank and overcrowded tenements that recall the description of industrialization in England in Victorian times. The automobile factories are less than 30 km away – glistening with machines and technology upgradations, clanking and hissing, where workers compete against robots. Moving faster and faster with diminishing pauses to eat and breathe, they conjure an image of *Modern Times*. The iconic Charlie Chaplin film where the combination of machine and impatient capital swallows the worker was shot in 1936 and captured contemporaneous reality. The film should have been an anachronism by now, except that it isn't, with labour extraction practices moving backwards in time to resemble the fictional reality.

While the two sectors – readymade garments and the automobile industry – appear starkly different, common to both is the increasing precarity. Greater informalization of labour, insecure employment, longer hours, removal of safeguards from the workplace, unhealthy intensification of work and inadequate rest have come together to result in a loss of hope for better lives.

STRETCH AND STRETCH:
THE CARROT AND STICK OF OVERTIME

Garments

'All week long, I wouldn't see daylight. I remember once, when things were slow, the foreman let us, girls, out in the middle of the day. 'What,' I said, 'are all the people on strike?' I never realized that so many people were out during the daytime.' – Clara Lemlich Shavelson, a young garment worker and leader of the Uprising of the Twenty Thousand in 1909, the historic New York City garment workers' strike that led to better working conditions.

The advent of the Industrial Revolution saw very long working hours in the newly established factories, with workers leaving home in the dark and returning after sunset, even during the long days of summer in the Northern hemisphere, rarely seeing the world in daylight. With factory owners keen to extract every millisecond of work from workers, there was little incentive to give periods of rest. While the nineteenth century saw a gradual reduction in the extraordinarily long hours of work (as much as 16 hours a day or 65 hours a week), the demand for an eight-hour working day became the focus of workers' struggles only in the late nineteenth century. It continued into the twentieth century until it became an established norm.

In 1919 the ILO's first convention was on limiting the working hours. Recognising that 'working excessive hours posed a danger to workers' health and their families', the convention decreed the maximum hours of work permissible: eight hours per day and no more than 48 hours per week. Since then, the eight-hour working day has become the global norm and has been adopted by most countries through domestic legislation. The universal acceptance of the limits of working hours finds expression in the concept of Overtime (OT), defined as working hours beyond the normal and requiring compensation well beyond the rate of remuneration offered for regular working hours.

India had ratified this ILO convention and enacted commensurate domestic legislation. Until recently, Section 59 of the Factories Act of 1948 governed overtime, entitling a worker to be paid at twice the rate of their ordinary rate of wages if the worker worked beyond the stipulated 48 hours a week. In theory, overtime is voluntary and is to be used in exceptional circumstances. In practice, as we shall see, it has become the norm, and the distinction between regular and overtime working hours has been all but erased.

Working beyond the scheduled hours is very common in the garment manufacturing industry. Overtime acts both as a compulsion and an incentive. The wages are so low that it is only through overtime that workers manage to make ends meet or save a little to send home. Even so, overtime is not entirely voluntary. The employer enforces it, and failing to show up for overtime can lead to dismissal or a threat of dismissal. Unwilling to keep a full workforce that could meet peak demand on their rolls, companies prefer to step pressure on their employees during times of high demand to meet the larger production targets. In the NCR belt, it is common to find workers staying in the factories till midnight and even working on Sundays from October onwards for several months. The peak festival season for India segues into the holiday season in the global North, making it a time of high demand for both the Indian and the overseas markets. Often, the workers do a minimum of 100 hours of overtime per month. Overtime is used regularly during periods of normal production as well. Fewer workers require less management, equipment, investment, and ancillary resources, thus cutting costs.

A peculiar method employed by some factories to exert pressure on workers is to employ a piece-rate worker and a time-rate worker in the same 'chain' or assembly line. The workers who are paid wages according to the number of pieces produced are interested in producing larger numbers of pieces, even if it means working more hours daily. This means that even time-rate workers are forced to work longer hours since both work interdependently on the same assembly line. A survey of garment workers in NCR, the results of which were published in a 2015 report authored by Alessandra Mezzadri and Ravi Srivastava, found that 'the average work hours were significantly higher in workshops (12.7 hours), followed by large and medium enterprises (9.7 and 9.6 hours respectively), with a lower 9.3 hours in small enterprises' (p. 121).

A large number of employers in the garment industry do not pay the legally stipulated rate for overtime or find other ways of shirking the payment. Some units pay double the rate for overtime work on Sundays but not on other days. The workers employed through labour contractors are more likely to be denied the higher rate for overtime. Companies also use various measures to fudge the calculation of hours put in as overtime. One such mechanism is to count only the first two hours after the regular shift as overtime, eligible for the double rate. Women usually do less overtime, but a larger proportion is likely to remain uncompensated for their extra hours.

Sohanlal came to Delhi in 2005 from Bhagalpur. He got a job as a thread cutter in Khandsa near Manesar for a monthly salary of Rs 2,400 through a labour contractor. Although his scheduled shift was supposed to be eight hours (excluding the lunch break), he and other workers would often start work in the morning and keep working till 9 or 10 pm. Occasionally, they worked till 1 am and sometimes even 5 am. For overtime work, Sohanlal was paid what is termed as 'single overtime' – the same rate as the normal working hours. Only those workers directly employed by the company were paid double the rate. Two years later, Sohanlal shifted to a garment company in Udyog Vihar, Gurgaon, which produced predominantly for exports. This was a large unit with 1000 workers. Sohanlal's earnings went up to Rs 5,600 per month, but they paid overtime at a single rate. He made another shift in 2009 and joined a reputed garment factory in Udyog Vihar. The company paid at the stipulated double rate but only for the first two hours. They paid overtime exceeding two hours at a single rate.

Not all are so lucky. Ramdin, a tailor in a fabricator unit in Udyog Vihar, does embroidery work on cushions and curtains. According to him, working 12-15 hours a day is standard, with no double rate for overtime. Starting from October, once the busy season starts, he logs in around 16-17 hours of work every day.

Elsewhere it is the nature of the contract that determines the pay. Suraj from Bhagalpur worked with a garment exporting company in Udyog Vihar till 2018. In his company, the second shift, which was supposed to get over by 9 pm or 10 pm, often extended up to 1 am during the festival season. According to Suraj, the workers employed directly by the company received double overtime, but those employed through the labour contractors received overtime at a single rate.

Adequate monetary compensation for overtime is the primary demand of the workers. The notion that eight hours of work should accord them a living wage that does not require them to work overtime is rarely mentioned. The idea that workers should have leisure time to sleep, eat, spend time with their families and even fulfil personal and domestic chores does not even enter the conversation. However, they talk about the exhaustion from overwork and the cumulative wear and tear of their bodies which shorten their working lives.

Automobiles

In the automobile sector, there is a wide variation in the working norms and adherence to labour laws. The OEMs – the brand companies, have relatively better working conditions. While the OEMs usually maintain eight-hour shifts and pay the stipulated overtime rates where required, their vendor companies use overtime extensively. They do not follow the legally mandated stipulations on time or payment, sometimes under pressure from the OEMs. For example, MSIL follows the eight-hour shift. Workers are usually required to stay back an extra hour only if the daily production target has not been met. However, with the coming in of global suppliers and increased competition amongst the suppliers in the late 1990s, Maruti began exerting pressure on existing vendors to reduce their cost of production. One way of lowering the cost was to have longer workdays for the vendor companies.

There are different working conditions for different workers within the vendor companies as well. The SPM Autocomp Systems Pvt Ltd, which manufactures exhaust manifold and steering knuckle, among other auto parts, supplies to many OEMs, including

Maruti, and has a foundry and a machine shop in Manesar. According to a November 2017 report, the foundry was manned by unskilled workers (PUDR 2017). Of the nearly 350 workers, only a handful were regular employees of the company; the rest were employed on a contractual basis through labour contractors. More than 80 per cent of the workers in the Machine Shop, where workers are often graduates from ITIs, were found to be regular workers. The workers in the machine shop worked eight-hour shifts and had a weekly holiday, while those in the foundry had twelve-hour shifts despite the work being more exhausting. They did not receive a weekly holiday. They were penalized by being kept out of the factory for several days if they missed a shift, thus missing substantive wages.

As will be seen in Chapter 5 and Annexure I, the new labour codes may worsen the situation for workers as they obfuscate the distinction between regular hours and overtime. For instance, the Code on Wages mandates that the preparatory work, though outside the normal working day, shall not be treated as overtime and hence not be eligible for overtime rate.

THE HUNGRY MACHINE: CEASELESS TOIL

Labour needs leisure. Workers need rest, breaks and nourishment in an otherwise monotonous and gruelling workday. For employers, on the other hand, time is money and squeezing the leisure time of workers is a strategy for increasing production. The blurring of boundaries between work and leisure time is reminiscent of factories and sweatshops of nineteenth-century Europe.

Consider the example of a well-known MNC's subsidiary unit in Noida. Although not engaged in garment or automobile production, this offers a striking illustration of how workers' break periods are squeezed further and further.

Sushila Devi has been employed for twenty years. Until a few years ago, her shift used to begin at 9 am. However, now, the production line starts at 8:45 am. As a routine, the production carries on till 10 minutes after 6 pm, which is the official time for the end of the shift. Further, the scheduled tea breaks (two in a day) have been reduced to 10 minutes each instead of the earlier 15 minutes. Each worker puts in 25-40 minutes of extra work almost daily (15 minutes before 9 am, 10 minutes after 6 pm and 10 minutes of reduced breaks). This extra time is not paid for.

Maruti's Manesar plant witnessed a year-long struggle by the workers in 2011 to form a union and improve working conditions. One important demand had been to increase the time for tea breaks. Before 2011 (and the union struggle), workers would only get a break of 7.5 minutes in which they were supposed to rush to the canteen, queue up, get their tea, have tea, and rush back to the production line.

'We got two tea breaks of seven minutes each in which we would rush to the canteen 150 metres away and back, and use this break to go to the toilet too, holding the teacup and snack in one hand even inside the toilet. There was a 30-minute lunch break. We would walk 300 metres to queue up for food, and rush back to the work stations to be there a minute before time.' – Maruti worker Iman Khan (Yadav 2015)

In Newsclick's 2011 documentary, *Maruti Workers' Strike – V for Victory*, which explored the working conditions inside the plant, one worker said they were not even allowed to go to the toilet outside the scheduled breaks.

Whether it is a lack of rest during each working day or a lack of rest day during the week, extracting more work out of a worker tends to make the worker resemble a machine rather than a person. The intensity comes not just from the ceaseless work but also the repetitive nature of the actions and the toll this takes on the human body.

Squeezing out the last drop of labour

'The animal has been surveyed and laid off like a map; and then the men have been classified in thirty specialities and twenty rates of pay, from 16 cents to 50 cents an hour. The 50-cent man is restricted to using the knife on the most delicate parts of the hide (floorman) or to using the axe in splitting the backbone (splitter); and wherever a less-skilled man can be slipped in at 18 cents, 18.5 cents, 20 cents, 21 cents, 22.5 cents, 24 cents, 25 cents, and so on, a place is made for him, and an occupation mapped out.'– Braverman (1974/2006: 56) quotes a description given by J.R. Commons of the first assembly line in American industry, the meatpacking conveyor.

'Taylorism' is a term familiar to management school students. The term expresses the 'scientific-management' techniques initiated by Frederick Winslow Taylor in the last decades of the nineteenth century to extract the maximum work from labour. For Taylor, 'a fair day's work' means 'all the work, a worker can do without injury to his health at a pace that can be sustained throughout a working lifetime' (Braverman 1974/2006:67). Taylor expounded principles of control over the workers in such a way that execution of work becomes tightly controlled by the managers.

By doing one small and rigidly defined piece of work instead of using complex skills, the workers' repetitive moves can be timed to a fraction of a second, and a high level of managerial control can be used to ensure its unceasing repetition at the fastest possible rate. Labour organizations have criticized Taylorism for turning the worker into an 'automaton' or 'machine,' making work monotonous and unfulfilling. Taylor's methods are reflected in control over the pace of work in today's industries. Assembly-line-based division of labour creates the possibility of increasing the pace of work. The division of labour is such that every worker in the assembly line is responsible for working on a small part of the product. This means that if the speed of the line could be enhanced, all workers would have to work faster.

Further, if some workers in the assembly line could be given incentives to work faster, others would be forced to keep pace. Conversely, some workers may be forced to do more intensified work processes by their terms of employment. This essentially makes the worker work faster or put in more labour/effort per unit of time. These methods are now regularly used in industrial units in India. For instance, the pace of work in the Maruti factory is described as follows.

> . . . if the assembly line halts, signboards across the shop floor light up – flashing the number of the workstation where the line has stopped and the duration of the stoppage. Another board displays the total time 'lost' during the shift; a scrolling ticker lists the production targets at a given time of the day, the actual cars produced and the variance. For every fault, the feedback is recorded, and the worker has to sign against it. It goes into his record. Every Maruti worker must sign Standing Orders that, among 100 other conditions, bar them from slowing down work, singing, gossiping, spreading rumours and making derogatory statements against the company and management. (Jha and Chakraborty 2012)

Companies have also used production-linked wage payments to increase the intensity of work. In Maruti, a considerable part of the wages, termed incentive wage, is linked to production. The form and method of calculation of incentive wages have changed over the years, but the underlying principle is unaltered. Intensifying the workload by increasing the speed can increase production if more and more is extracted faster and faster from the worker. Here, wasted time is measured in fractions of seconds using managerial and mechanical means. There is little cost to the company if this punitive pace shortens the worker's working life. Workers can be replaced quickly and cheaply, unlike machinery.

Within a month of joining an automobile OEM, Mohan's soles were badly swollen as he had to move to and from a distance of 10-12 feet to put nuts and bolts for a car seat. This happened continuously and relentlessly for 450 cars in one day. '*Aadmi nichur jaata hai*' (A man is completely wrung out) after an 8-hour shift, he told me, explaining why he felt compelled to leave the coveted job at a global auto giant.

In its extreme form, there can be demands to increase production by as much as 50 per cent without any investment. This took an extreme form in 2010 in Maruti. The company experienced a demand surge and tried to meet this without investing in an additional assembly line. This led to massive intensification, and production at the Gurgaon plant rose by 17 per cent and at the Manesar plant by 40 per cent (Jha and Chakraborty 2012). The maximum burden of increased intensification fell on the contract workers.

How untenable this was, became evident from the year-long workers' agitation in 2011 for forming a union and for better working conditions. As mentioned earlier, one significant demand was increasing tea break time. After the 2011 struggle, the tea breaks were doubled, and the break time became 15 minutes.

The use of mechanical and managerial means for increasing production is not confined to the more technology-intensive automobile industry. To supervise and increase the work intensity in the garment industry, factories deploy devices such as stopwatches and magnetic cards.

As a result of the decomposition and fragmentation of manufacturing processes, companies employing Taylorist methods can hire workers with lesser skills and training. This enlarges the pool of potential workers for them and contributes to lowering of wages. The worker is a *tool* in executing jobs on the assembly line.

In Udyog Vihar's garment sector, under the 'chain system,' each worker is responsible for a small part of the work, such as stitching the collar or one arm of the shirt. Not surprisingly, skilled artisans have become replaceable and substitutable by trainees with a few weeks of learning how to operate sewing machines.

The repetitive work, where the same physical motions are repeated hundreds of times without pause, also results in muscle injuries and physical burnout, rarely addressed as workplace injuries. 'Men don't survive very long in the export line. Our eyes are the first casualty. My eyes have become weak over the years,' Jaichand, a garment worker, told me. His factory had 15-20 production lines, and each line had about 25-30 machines. Each machine/ worker is expected to produce 30 pieces (of cuff, or collar, or one part of the shirt) in an hour.

Speed and the need for cutting costs related to health and safety cause other severe injuries and problems but are treated as aberrations rather than the outcome of the working process. According to a civil society report, 'The main health risk undoubtedly comes from the nature of work – requiring focused attention and fixed postures, as well as long hours . . . Dust and particle pollution is regarded by workers as the main cause of health risk in the garment industry (i.e., by 79 per cent of workers across all firms), followed by eye strain (39.1 per cent of all workers). Accidents are regarded as a smaller but a significant source of health risk, with 7.9 per cent of workers perceiving these to be the major health risk' (Mezzadri and Srivastava 2015: 128). The report further pointed out workers are not provided with safety equipment in the workshops.

ACCIDENTS AND ABUSE

Investment in safety equipment is not uniform. Smaller units often forgo the safety standards, measures, and equipment. On 23 November 2015, at least five workers were grievously injured because of a fire on the upper floor of the M/S Fashion Global Limited, Gurgaon unit. The factory workers claimed the fire was caused by a boiler bursting on the upper floor. However, the supervisor and a management representative said there was no boiler in the factory. One explanation could be that the unit did not have the license to use the boiler.

Such incidents are far too 'minor' to cause any disruption in the production routine. It is only when accidents occur on the scale of the Rana Plaza disaster in Bangladesh that it draws the international gaze. The collapse of the eight-storey commercial building resulted in the death of more than 1100 people. It led to big brands declaring their social conscience by temporarily ceasing to buy from Bangladesh. Undoubtedly the purchasers moved to a more convenient place for producing garments under similar sweatshop conditions.

In some cases, the production pressure is such that workers themselves dispense with personal safety equipment. In a garment unit in Udyog Vihar, I was told that although safety gear such as finger guards and plastic footwear is provided to prevent electrocution, the production targets are such that workers make do without the gear to save time. The increasing pace of work and consequent pressure to lower safeguards creates a situation where industrial accidents have become more commonplace.

Orient Craft, a leading readymade garment exporter, monitors individual tailors with stopwatches and reinforces the monitoring with magnetic card readers that relay data on the number of seconds it takes each worker to finish a piece. According to a report by seven Delhi-based democratic rights and labour rights organizations, on 28 March 2014, a 35-year-old tailor, Sunil, died at work in a Gurgaon unit of the company. The workers claimed that the cause of death was electrocution, whereas the management attributed the death to a heart attack. This accident fuelled violent clashes between the police and the workers for two consecutive days. The report concluded that irrespective of the proximate cause

Introduction of machines
Its impact on the workforce

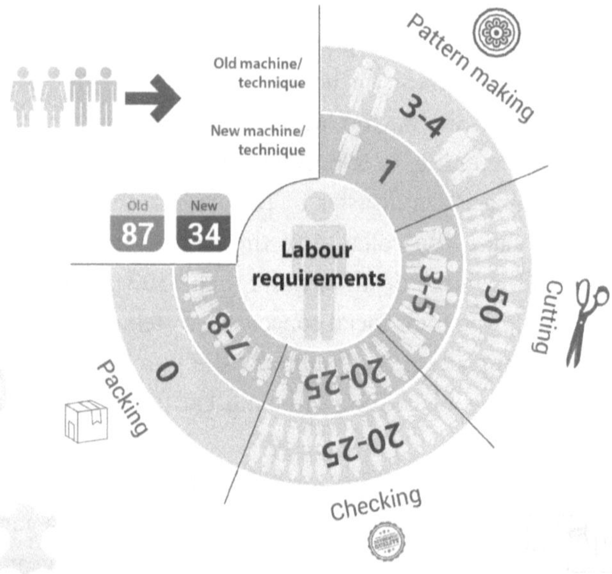

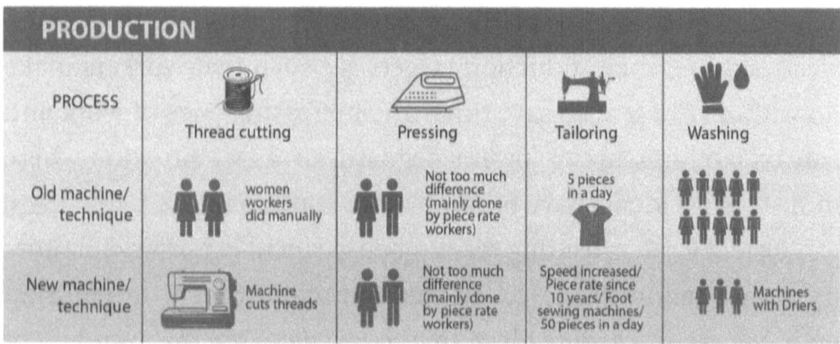

Source: Interview with a garment worker in Udyog Vihar in 2019

of death, almost everyone admitted to terrible work conditions and continuous increase in work intensity.[1] What was shocking

---

[1] Report of a fact-finding team (2014), *Hum Ko Bacha Lo: Death of a Worker in Gurgaon*, Inquilabi Mazdoor Kendra (IMK), Krantikari Naujawan Sabha (KNS), Mazdoor Patrika, Perspectives, People's Union for Democratic Rights (PUDR), Sanhati, and Workers' Unity. http://sanhati.com/articles/9560/

was that the work intensity was so high that the workers working alongside the deceased did not even realize that he had collapsed till some time had lapsed.

The desire for cost-saving can result in grotesque outcomes. On 6 April 2017, Shatrughan, a 24-year-old contract *safai karamchari* (cleaner), was accidentally stuck in the belt in the SPM factory's foundry at Manesar at 5.30 am, according to a report by PUDR. At 7 am, other workers came to know of it, and they demanded to speak with the management to cut the belt to rescue Shatrughan. However, the management did not allow this, as cutting the belt would have been a cost to the company. Though the workers resorted to a 'tool down,' Shatrughan was finally removed to safety much later in the day. Shatrughan died of his injuries in the hospital later that day. An FIR was lodged against many of the protesting workers.

During PUDR's investigation, the workers reported frequent accidents. A worker had suffered an eye injury during work, another worker's finger was cut off, and another's arm got entangled in the conveyor belt. In such cases, the company paid for a one-time treatment, but no compensation was paid. They said there was rarely any compensation for workers who were injured. Unless the injury is serious, there is no support even for the treatment. The period to recover from the injury is considered unpaid leave. When workers re-join, they are expected to resume work with the same intensity and pace. They can always be replaced easily. Workers attribute frequent accidents to excessive workload. A terminated worker from Vertical Machine Control (VMC) said that within five years, the production target in a single shift almost doubled from 60 pieces to 110 pieces. And this was done without changing the machines physically but simply by increasing the speed of the machines.

The idea that machines should not have any 'idle time' is carried on to the extent that machines are not stopped even for maintenance work. In other cases, a consequence of technological upgradation is increasing control of the work process on the shop floor. With no job security, workers who attempt to unionize or raise issues related to working conditions are the first to go. A resulting outcome of this has been the inability of workers to bargain for better working conditions. Workers who protest find themselves facing criminal charges. Workers now rely on the protections secured through their collective struggles. How robust are these protections? In Chapter 5, we turn to the safeguards provided by labour laws and the recent legislative reforms that have altered this landscape.

5. From Protecting to Disciplining Labour: A Short History of Labour Laws

No sunlight, no ventilation, and 16-hour working days on the factory floor. No health and safety measures, verbal and physical abuse, and children as young as four toiling inside in dark and dingy rooms. As Britain began to industrialize in the eighteenth century, thousands of workers poured into British factories each day. Owners sought to extract the maximum by way of profits through exploitation of the labour force, leading to abysmal working conditions. There were no limits on the number of hours, no restrictions on the working conditions inside the factories, or the worker's minimum age, let alone any measure to ensure their mental and physical well-being. Fourteen to sixteen hours of work was the standard, as was the employment of young children. Wages were so low as to be insufficient for the vast majority of workers to meet the bodily needs of their families.

It was in response to these sub-human working conditions that the early laws regulating working conditions, i.e., labour laws, were formulated in the nineteenth and early twentieth centuries, establishing a minimum level of protection for workers, limiting the number of hours of work and the worker's age, along with the institutionalization of other health and safety measures.

As industrialization spread, replicating similar, if not worse, abysmal working conditions in different countries, protests by workers erupted. The ensuing struggles led to the establishment of laws. The passage of the laws was however not without stiff opposition from industrialists, and the progress in securing rights was slow and incremental. The body of legislation today termed labour laws emerged in a piecemeal fashion to act as an arbiter between the industrialists' desire for profit and the worker's desire for a decent standard of living. Over time, however, some of the laws which provided essential protections to labour acquired the standing of a universally agreed social compact. Given the inherent inequality between employers and employees, the laws gained acceptance to ensure the principles of natural justice. They recognized that the marketplace alone could not be the sole determinant of working conditions, focusing mainly on profit maximization and extraction of the maximum possible work with little consideration for the worker.

However, the struggles that led to these laws are far from over. While some countries have widened the ambit of progressive legislation, in other parts of the world, the powerful push back against these laws has succeeded in ensuring a steady roll-back of some essential protections. The reversal has been achieved through avoidance of implementation of the laws by using loopholes or flouting the laws with the backing of political influence, money and muscle power, especially in places where there is a weak rule of law. The growing clout of industry and corporations over political power has also enabled the dilution of the social compact on a minimum standard of living, even as the areas exempted from the laws – determined both geographically and by the nature of the industry – have grown steadily. Over time, this has allowed for the repeal and replacement of many of the laws, with new legislation based on industry interests rather than those of labour.

WORKERS' STRUGGLES AND THE EMERGING
LABOUR LAW REGIME

During the early phases of industrialization, mills, which originated in England and then spread to Belgium, France, Switzerland, Germany, and the United States, primarily employed immigrant workers, including women and children. Employers wanted to extract the maximum possible work from these workers. Thus, the core of the modern working class was formed in the conditions of misery and oppression. Extremely severe mill regulations, fines, wage reductions, dismissals, long working hours, sicknesses, and accidents were common. However, harsh work conditions also provided the push for the formation of collective worker organizations. Workers' struggles in the nineteenth century 'were often acts of men and women driven by misery and hunger . . . in order to survive' rather than an outcome of organized resistance (Beaud 1981/2004: 113). There were spontaneous explosions of rage as well as more long-drawn efforts to form workers' organizations. Workers' struggles and organizations exerted pressure on the employers and society at large. Some of the demands became recognized as fundamental rights in due course of time.

England granted universal male suffrage in 1867. The Trades Union Congress was founded in the subsequent year. France recognized the 'right to strike' in 1864. Similarly, in Germany, the constitution of 1867 established universal suffrage. Workers' movements grew in other European countries and the United States. The first large, centralized US trade union, the National Labour Union, was founded in 1866. The International Workingmen's Association, founded in 1864, sought to forge international solidarity amongst workers and their organizations. Strikes and struggles broke out among different sections of workers in these countries at the end of the nineteenth century. Railroad workers, miners, weavers, glassmakers and textile workers asserted their rights as workers and citizens and forced employers to grant concessions.

Legislatures in Europe and North America were forced to enact laws to protect the interests of the labouring classes. In Britain, the Employers and Workmen Act of 1875 replaced the Master and Servant Act of 1867. Laws in 1875 and 1876 gave trade unions legal status. Laws related to medical and accident insurance as well as old age benefits, were passed in Germany around the same time. France passed laws granting freedom of association regarding the length of the working day, weekly rest for workers and workplace safety. Many states adopted laws ensuring an eight-hour working day in the United States. Social acceptance of many demands put forth by workers was, in effect, an acceptance of the natural principles of justice. The history of May Day is also linked to the demand for an eight-hour working day.

The increasing political strength of workers' organizations increased their bargaining power vis-à-vis employers. This new balance of forces explained: 'the conquest and new benefits which came to the working world' (Beaud 1981/ 2004: 149). As a result, real wages increased across the industrial world, the length of the working day reduced, and working conditions improved compared to the beginning of the nineteenth century.

Global protections for labour in the post-War period

The next shift in the global labour law regime came after the Second World War. Growing strength of the Soviet Union, pressures of the Cold War and the institution of the International Labour Organisation (ILO) contributed towards this. In time, some of the fundamental laws for labour protection were enshrined as part of the Universal Declaration of Human Rights. Embedded in the early legislation on workers' rights was the acceptance of two fundamental principles – that 'labour is not a commodity', enshrined through the 1944 Philadelphia Declaration of the ILO, and that workers had the 'right to collective bargaining', later codified through legislation legalising trade unions. These principles were an implicit recognition of the unequal power of the employer and the employee. Without regulation, the employer could attempt to maximize profits by paying lower and lower wages, withholding job security, and not meeting health and safety requirements. Without the right to use collective action, an individual employee would have no means or strength to negotiate with the employer on any of these issues, however just the cause.

A widespread consensus evolved around working conditions such as safety, minimum age, and a ban on child labour in hazardous work. Yet, there was considerable continual disagreement among economists on 'employment and wage flexibility'.[1] At the heart of flexibility in employment is employers' freedom to hire and fire depending on the demand and supply of labour. Wage flexibility argues that wages are determined by the 'free markets' without the constraints imposed by trade unions or minimum wage legislation. For industrialists, wages are viewed as the most easily controlled cost of production to maintain or increase profits. If the supply of labour is sufficient, cheaper and cheaper labour could be used for the same amount of work. Similarly, employment of part-time or temporary labour allows the industrialists to regulate the use of quantum of labour in accordance with demand. Articulated as the theory of 'free and flexible labour markets', this theory views labour as a market commodity.

History has been marked by periods when market forces dominated thinking and policy, alternating with periods when there was a spread of institutions to regulate the market outcomes. The 'flexibility' view argued that workers were 'free' to take employment as the employers were to hire them. However, this 'truth' is more nominal than substantive. Although employers and workers are mutually dependent on each other, the relationship is defined by inequality. Low wages – a product of the marketplace

---

[1] The debate is an old one although the usage of the term 'flexibility' has been prevalent since the 1980s.

– do not allow the workers to build a buffer that can sustain them through long periods of layoffs. Unrestricted working hours do not allow them time to rest and recuperate, let alone take care of their families. Lack of job security keeps them in a constant state of anxiety and prevents them from planning any betterment of their lives. Bad working conditions destroy their health. Thus, workers' productive years end well before their natural course. While 'labour market flexibility' has developed into a robust economic theory, it is pertinent that this principle is applied generally to blue-collar workers, the lowest rung of the industrial workforce and the most vulnerable one. While contractual jobs have replaced permanent employment in a large section of the white-collar jobs, they are well-regulated, providing predictable tenures, safety and other workplace features related to well-being, and financial compensation in lieu of permanent employment.

UNFULFILLED PROMISES?

In India, some of the most significant labour laws were enacted in the colonial period, the first of which was the Factory Act of 1881. Its adoption was also influenced by the Lancashire mill owners, who were not keen on mill owners in India having an unfair advantage after they had been forced to create more humane working conditions in the British factories. As in other parts of the world, there were strikes and struggles by the workers in India, such as the Bombay Cotton Mills workers' seven-month-long strike in 1928 and the Ahmedabad textile workers' strike in the 1930s. The colonial government responded to industrial strikes by passing the Industrial Disputes Act of 1947, the last labour-related law passed by the colonial regime. This Act laid down provisions and procedures for prior government permission for laying off workers and extensive provisions for the government as an adjudicator. Although amended several times, this Act stayed in place until it was superseded in 2020 by the Industrial Relations Code.

Other significant legislations were also enacted during the colonial period between 1926 and 1947 – for example, the Trade Union Act, Industrial Employment (Standing Orders) Act, Workmen's Compensation Act, and the Payment of Wages Act. State intervention and adjudication were essential aspects of early labour laws, but there was also an explicit aim of curbing collective bargaining. The Industrial Disputes Act gave enormous power to the government to declare some industries as public utilities, forcing industrial disputes for conciliation and adjudication and prohibiting strikes and lockouts during the conciliation and adjudication process. The Statement of Object and Reasons accompanying the original 1947 bill shows how government intervention was aimed toward curbing collective bargaining:

'The power to refer disputes of Industrial Tribunals and enforce their awards is an essential corollary to the obligation that lies on the government to secure conclusive determination of the disputes to redress the legitimate grievances of the parties thereto, such obligation arising from the imposition of restraints on the right of strike and lockout, *which must remain inviolate*, except where considerations of public interest override such rights' (Mohapatra 2015).

The early objective becomes important in light of future developments. There was hope that the early laws would be enlarged and amplified over time, as has been the case for a substantive body of laws relating to human rights. However, this did not happen. The history of labour-related legislation in the seven decades since India became a republic is not linear. While industrialists used 'rationalization' and 'restructuring' as the twin tools to increase their profitability, reduce wages, and exempt themselves from the existing provisions of laws, workers' collective action secured significant additional rights. State intervention occasionally worked in favour of workers, while a pro-business attitude in the polity also undermined many existing rights. Over time as the profession of socialist principles gave way to an assertive practice of neoliberal politics, the haemorrhaging of rights acquired pace. 'Ease of business', 'labour market flexibility', 'investment opportunity' and 'zones of exception' became the new mantras. The hoped-for strengthening of laws that would act as a fair arbiter of contradictory needs of workers and management did not take place, belying the expectation of 'progressive application' through national laws.

Nor has India adopted measures of social welfare that are provided in many developed countries to provide a subsistence level of support and safety nets. Contrary to the professed goal of providing a greater proportion of the workforce with better jobs and an ability to move beyond the economic situation they were born into, a greater proportion of the job creation was of jobs that were in the unorganized and unregulated sector. At the same time, the regulated sector too moved towards the use of contract labour, short-term employment, and use of casual workers, thus reducing the expenditure on labour. This was starkly visible during Covid when thousands of migrant workers (including some industrial workers) were forced to walk, some for thousands of kilometres, because they had no means, no savings, and no buffer to stay in the cities where they had provided labour, some of them for their entire lifetime. There was little succour for them.

Labour market reforms

Globally as well as in India, social sanction and sensibility regarding certain labour protections for labour were steadily withdrawn after the 1970s. The reasons for this are outside the scope of this book. The governments and policymakers started undermining union power, collective bargaining, and state adjudication alongside increasing emphasis on free markets. The labour market throughout the world became more 'flexible', resulting in the rise of insecure and low-paying jobs. Of course, there were differences across countries, and continental Europe tried to preserve some social protection for the workers, although accompanied by high levels of unemployment. Global corporations dispersed and outsourced production and assembling to cheaper locations, such as India.

Within India, the sensibility of the state towards labour began to change in official policy as well. Economic reforms were accompanied by an emphasis on labour market reforms. Even before 1991, 'labour flexibility' was introduced in practice without formal legislative measures. The state withdrew from industrial relations, and the power of trade unions weakened. Labour laws began to be viewed as an impediment by the factory owners and the state. The next few decades would see the state intervening less and less in favour of the workers, diluting labour protections, and finally actively intervening in favour of the owners. The existing laws were observed more in the breach. The Second National Commission on Labour (SNCL) 2002, appointed by the Government of India, clearly states a key task of the Commission as 'to suggest rationalization of existing laws relating to labour in the organized sector' (Roychowdhury 2018: 1). Over time, provisions of the Industrial Disputes Act have been treated as chief stumbling blocks to making the labour markets less rigid. Economic Survey of 2005-06 talked of the labour laws being highly protective of labour, thus obstructing competitiveness and economic growth while restricting employment in the organized sector. The laws were deemed a deterrent to the employers who would not hire if they did not have the freedom to dispense with the workers. One way in which even the scant protections of the legal regime have been effectively undermined is by ensuring that most of the workforce lies outside the ambit of the labour laws.

INADEQUATE, YET INVALUABLE

The labour laws are applied differentially to different parts of the workforce. Most of the laws apply only to a fraction of the workforce – i.e., those employed in industries registered with the government, which employ permanent workers, and have a workforce of a certain size. The number of workers in this category is small, but its significance lies beyond the sheer numbers. The quality of jobs assured by applying the whole gamut of laws is significantly better than that of the bulk of workers in the informal, unorganized sector. However, the organized sector's importance is aspirational, the dream of a better livelihood and better lives that workers could aspire to if they have sufficient skills and if they work hard. It demonstrates the protections that could be extended over time to encompass the entire workforce as society advances.

However, the dream of better-quality jobs that allow for a life of sufficiency and upliftment over generations has been undermined by reality. On the one hand, the growth in the manufacturing sector jobs has been limited. On the other, the jobs that have been created have moved from organized and regulated to informal jobs. The bulk of jobs are low-paying, requiring minimal skills, ensuring that workers have no opportunity of moving up, thus, remaining stuck in a cycle of insecurity, low wages, and ad hoc employment over their entire lifetime.

In 2012-13, more than half the workers (58.7 per cent) in the organized manufacturing sector in our country were not governed by the labour laws, and the trend has been increasing since 2003-04 (Roychowdhury 2018: 79).[2] The situation of workers employed

---

[2] Establishments employing fewer than 100 workers were outside the ambit of labour laws till recently. Number of regular workers in the 0-100 category along with contract workers gives the figure of 58.7 per cent. With the coming of new labour codes, the percentage would rise. Industrial Relations Code, 2020 states that factories and enterprises employing less than 300 workers will not require government permission for retrenching workers or lockout of the firm.

in the unorganized manufacturing sector has been even worse.

Laws in practice

While job creation has placed jobs outside the regulated sphere, there has also been significant relaxation in the regulations themselves. For example, the threshold for industries that are required to take permission for retrenching employees has increased from 50 to 300. The result has been an exponential growth in the number of non-permanent contractual employees and horizontal segmentation of companies to stay below the threshold to comply with the letter of the law while avoiding its intent. Similarly, while the law imposed restrictions on the retrenchment of employees in continuous employment, employers chose to break the period of continuous employment by laying off workers before the maximum number of days and re-employing them after a gap of a few days.

There is growth in the number of workers employed on contract despite the Contract Labour (Regulation and Abolition) Act 1970. This Act's objective was to prevent contract workers' exploitation and abolish the contract labour system where permanent employees could do the work. Instead of employer compliance, the Act places the burden on a worker's proactivity to enforce his rights. This gap in the law has been the fertile ground for contract labour growth in India. The Act places no penalties on the employer for employing contract labour and, in effect, encourages him to subvert the provisions of other labour laws by employing contractual workers.

The rapid retreat of governments from their obligations to the workforce has enabled the impunity for such avoidance and non-implementation of laws. The government machinery for enforcing laws and regulations has been diluted. The tribunals set up to adjudicate have been enfeebled. The political will has moved en masse in support of the employer, not the worker, guised in the catch phrases of labour market 'flexibility', 'investment-friendly' and 'pro-industry'.

From the second half of the 1980s, the managerial class launched a political offensive against the existing unions. Instead of reaching a settlement with them, managers began presenting a 'charter of demands' to *their unions* wherein they dictated terms such as workforce reduction, linking wages to productivity, and freedom to employ contract labour. Victimization of trade union activists, imposition of illegal lockouts, and coerced 'voluntary' retirement became common.[3] Government authorities, very often, colluded with the management.

The only potentially reparative force, that of workers' collective action, has been weakened considerably by a combination of factors: the lack of permanent employment, the subversion of large labour unions by political parties, and where both these have failed, workers' collective action to demand their dues has been characterized as a law-and-order problem that requires quelling through forceful policing, criminalization and subsequent legal action. The garment and automobile industry in the NCR provides tangible evidence of the entire gamut of approaches, from avoidance of law and lack of collective action to the law-and-order approach to dealing with workers' demands.

LAWS AND LIVES IN THE GARMENT AND AUTOMOBILE INDUSTRIES

Garments

There have been no significant unionization or workers' struggles in the NCR's garment sector. There have been sporadic

---

[3] A lockout is a work stoppage or denial of employment initiated by the management during a labour dispute. In contrast to a strike, in which employees refuse to work, a lockout is initiated by employers or industry owners. The Supreme Court has clearly stated that the use of weapons by the respective parties must be subject to the relevant provisions of the Industrial Disputes Act.

worker struggles, typically in response to specific situations like an accident. One possible reason could be the fluidity of employment. The workers are rarely employed in a specific factory for a long time. They keep shifting from one factory to the other, from one plot number to another. Once or twice a year, many of them travel back to their villages. Upon return, they may or may not be absorbed in the same factory. This essentially means that there is not too much of a sense of a collective within a particular factory. Another reason for the lack of unionization is the insecure nature of jobs and long work hours.

An accident at Orient Craft Limited in 2014 claimed Sunil Pushkar's life. After Sunil had been taken to the hospital, workers gathered in large numbers outside the factory gate. Assistant Sub-Inspector Jaipal Singh said that the police received information of workers gathering around noon, and they sent 65 policemen from different stations to the factory gate 'to avert any trouble'. When workers realized that Sunil had died, they were angry and demanded that his body should be returned to them. They feared the management would hush up the death or file a false report to avoid liability and compensation. Such instances are not unheard of in the garment factories of Udyog Vihar. According to a worker, two general managers of the company told them, 'What will you do with the body? Why don't you settle for compensation?' Workers were furious on hearing this and got into a scuffle with the management officials. The police responded with lathi charge and tear gas shells, and workers pelted bricks and stones at the police officials. Workers were chased back to their residential quarters in Sarhaul village, and police broke into some rooms and beat up the occupants. According to newspaper reports, nearly two dozen people, including workers and police officers, were injured in clashes that day. A local newspaper reported that Assistant Commissioner of Police Balwan Singh filed a First Information Report against factory workers.

The survey of the garment workers of NCR showed that less

than 2 per cent (1.7 per cent) of the workers had any written contract (Mezzadri and Srivastava 2015:108). Not a single worker surveyed admitted being part of any union. When asked why they had not joined a union, almost half of the workers said that they were apprehensive of the consequences, while a quarter simply said that they were not interested, but 28 per cent pointed out that there were no unions in their area, or none had approached them . . . Only about a third of the workers (31.8 per cent) were in favour of unions being formed at their work places. (Mezzadri and Srivastava 2015:152).

However, this situation in NCR is not emblematic of garment workers in other parts of the country. Early in June 2020, Euro Clothing Company Factory (ECC-2), a supplier of H&M owned by Gokaldas Exports in Srirangapatna (Karnataka), announced that more than 1000 workers were to be laid off immediately and the factory would no longer be operational. The management's notice said that this sudden closure was due to the global effects of the coronavirus pandemic. However, the factory workers were unionized and began protesting immediately and continued to do so even after weeks of the closure. Eight months after the workers were first laid off, the company agreed to re-employ them. While the Srirangapatna factory remains closed, the company had agreed to take workers back to a factory 12 km away from the one that was shut down. The workers' union, Garment and Textile Workers Union (GATWU), sought to enforce H&M's Global Framework Agreement (GFA) with the understanding that in the global supply chain, transnational corporations must bear responsibility for the rights of their suppliers' workers, too (Suresh and Bhat 2021).[4]

The garment industry in NCR has been restructuring itself to avoid coming under the ambit of labour laws. The laws relate to the size of the factory rather than the size of the firm. Many

---

[4] Also see the statement issued by New Trade Union Initiative accessed from https://ntui.org.in/?p=1862

firms grow 'horizontally' so that the size of individual factories (owned by the firm) remains small. Often, the number of workers is underreported to evade the law.

Automobiles

The situation in the automobile sector stands in sharp contrast in terms of unionization and workers' struggles. The NCR belt has seen some significant struggles. Automobile companies have often responded using force and intimidation. Struggles by workers of Rico Auto company (Gurgaon, 2009) and Maruti Suzuki (Manesar, 2011-2012) are well-known. From 2005-2009, the struggle for union formation, inspired by the Honda workers' struggle, spread to various plants in Gurgaon-Manesar-Dharuhera. Almost 35-40 unions were formed in this period in the auto belt. The permanent workers of the newly formed unions improved their salaries, facilities and working conditions, establishing a plant-level collective bargaining mechanism. In 2009, workers of the vendor company Rico Auto Limited (Gurgaon) were on strike for 44 days when management-hired goons (bouncers) opened fire at the factory gate and killed a worker, Ajit Yadav. This triggered massive anger in the entire belt. Thousands of workers took out rallies that culminated at the Rico factory gate. More than one lakh workers struck work for one day. But the plant-level leadership could not withstand the pressure from the management and the administration and resigned (Amit and Nayanjyoti 2018:8).

At the Manesar plants of MSIL, tensions were simmering regarding the differences in wages and treatment of workers employed under differing categories. These crystallized into a campaign to form a trade union for all workers, Maruti Suzuki Workers Union (MSWU). Management's refusal to recognize MSWU led to the first wave of conflict in 2011. The company terminated eleven worker leaders. This led to a sit-in and strike, and occupation of a part of the company by the workers.

Retrenched workers were reinstated, but MSWU was not recognized. The striking workers were asked to sign 'good conduct bonds' leading to a walk-out by MSWU and subsequent lockout by the management (see Annexure I for the text of the bond). Regular workers returned after a month, but many contract and casual workers were dismissed. The management agreed to one-off pay increases for most workers, moved towards recognition of MSWU provided it remained unaffiliated with any other national unions and provided that non-regular workers remained outside wage negotiations. At the same time, 100 police officers remained stationed at the site round the clock.

MSWU was recognized in March 2012, but the management clarified that most of the workers would not be regularized. On 18 July 2012, there was an argument between a worker and his supervisor and the worker was suspended. The union began negotiating with the human resources team at the plant. The management alleged that when the negotiations broke down without a compromise, violence erupted with workers attacking the staff, including senior officials, with iron rods and other objects. The workers strongly object to this position and claim that many private security personnel were already present inside the premises, instigating the violence. In the melee, a fire broke out on the campus and gutted down a section of the factory. The General Manager (HR), Awanish Kumar Dey, lost his life. What followed was a spate of dismissals and arrests of workers. A total of 546 regular workers and 1500 contract workers were retrenched. Around 148 workers were accused of murder and arrested. After a trial of around five years, the Sessions Court pronounced its judgment in March 2017, convicting 31 accused workers in the case. Of these, 13 were awarded life sentences. As the PUDR report states: 'This judgement has become a handy tool in the hands of managements of other automobile companies, and the resistant workers are constantly reminded of what happened to their Maruti brethren' (PUDR 2017: 5).

At the time of writing, workers have been released on bail pending their appeal before the High Court but only after spending considerable time in prison. Jia Lal, the union leader, died in custody in June 2021, and his family reported that his condition worsened due to a lack of adequate medical care for his spinal cancer.

More recently, Honda Motorcycle and Scooter India, Manesar is a telling illustration of evasion of obligations and culpability by lead automobile companies. In this case, the settlement with the retrenched and agitating contract workers was undertaken by the labour contractor and not HMSI (see also Chapter 3). Another strategy used by the automobile companies is to change the very organization of production and labour to make workers' struggles increasingly difficult. Companies set up multiple units to shift production to another unit without much loss if one unit witnesses workers' protests. Automation and mechanization have reduced the importance of workers' skills and experience. The nature of jobs has been becoming more insecure and more disposable. Permanent workers have been reduced to a minority in most companies. The management creates divisions among workers by giving generous pay hikes to a few amongst the workforce via collective wage agreements while excluding the majority of workers from such benefits. Nevertheless, the very existence of unions acts as a safety valve for the workers.

For Mohan, his factory's union is the only thing that stands between him and joblessness. He attributes the prevention of large-scale retrenchment in the Covid lockdown phase to the presence of the union. He spoke of around 170-250 workers of his company with seven-month contract jobs who were laid off because of the lockdown. He feels he and other non-permanent workers would have been thrown out of the jobs if not for the Union. In companies without a union, the 'situation is very bad'. 'It is only because of the union that we are free'.

FROM PROTECTING TO DISCIPLINING LABOUR

Law is being replaced by law-and-order with a greater emphasis on *order*. This has become easier with the changes in the organization of production and changes in the nature of jobs. New categories of workers like Diploma trainee, Student trainee, and Diploma Apprentices are not recognized as 'workers'. Strikes and mass protests are increasingly dealt with by the heavy hand of the police. Incidents of police 'lathi charge' on striking workers, foisting criminal cases, and incarceration are commonplace. Labour courts and departments have become less important as civil and criminal courts settle labour matters.

In many cases, worker termination is violative of the IDA provisions. But often, workers are not in a situation to challenge the same legally due to the absurdly lengthy legal process. Case after case, workers struggle to form unions, mired in labour departmental delays. This also provides time for the management to terminate the workers. Civil courts have become sufficiently pliant and easily grant a stay against the assembly of protesting workers inside the plant, within 100-500 meters of the factory gate at the time of workers' struggles, as in the case of HMSI.

The attitude of courts and judiciary can be seen in an earlier case involving the Maruti workers. Twenty-four workers who had been terminated in 2000 filed a case against the termination and won the case about five years later. But the court ordered no reinstatement as they were no longer fit for the new production regime and instead ordered compensation of a few lakh rupees (Amit and Nayanjyoti 2018: 29). While rejecting the bail plea of Maruti workers who had been arrested after the 2012 incident in Manesar, the Haryana High Court observed that 'The incident is a most unfortunate occurrence which has lowered the reputation of India in the estimation of the world. Foreign investors are not likely to invest money in India out of fear of labour unrest.' The manner of the prosecution and the slow pace of the trial led the

International Commission for Labour Rights to state that the labour department 'failed in its duty to serve as an impartial and effective administrative and adjudicators' body regarding labour matters' (Venkat T., Tadepalli, Manuel 2017).

De jure flexibility: New labour codes

The journey towards the erosion of worker protections and ever greater labour market flexibility has received a fillip with the passing of the new labour codes. The Ministry for Labour and Employment introduced four Labour Codes between 2019 and 2020, replacing 29 of the existing 44 labour laws. However, the labour codes have not yet been implemented, as the central and state governments have not formulated rules to make them operational. The four codes are:

a. Code on Wages, 2019: This replaced the earlier laws relating to wages and bonuses, that is, the Payment of Wages Act, 2019, the Minimum Wages Act 1948, the Payment of Bonus Act, 1965 and the Equal Remuneration Act, 1976.

b. Occupational Safety, Health and Working Conditions Code, 2020 (OSHWC Code): This replaced the Factory Act 1948, Contract Labour (Regulation and Abolition) Act 1970, among many others.

c. Industrial Relations Code, 2020 (IR Code): This replaced Industrial Disputes Act 1947, and Trade Union Act 1926, amongst others.

d. Social Security Code, 2020.

The Code on Wages can potentially affect the minimum wages adversely since it introduces the concept of a national floor wage. This code has also obfuscated the distinction between regular work hours and overtime work. The OSHWC Code further removes the maximum limit on overtime hours, thus paving the way for greater intensification of work in a day. Unlike the labour commissioners appointed under the previous legal regime, the labour inspectors-cum-facilitators have the dual responsibility of facilitating investment and resolving disputes, thus creating a conflict of interest. In a cruel inversion of accountability, the OSHWC Code has a clause potentially penalising the worker for industrial accidents if they fail to 'take reasonable care' or 'cooperate with the employer in meeting statutory obligations'. On the other hand, safety mechanisms to prevent industrial accidents have been diluted by this code. The Social Security Code has, for the first time, included gig workers, platform workers, home-based and self-employed workers within its purview. However, it remains to be seen if the commitments made towards informal workers are actually undergirded by financial resources and effective implementation mechanisms.

The Industrial Relations Code has the potential to undo many hitherto existing protections won through long years of workers' struggles. The role of the right to organize, strike, and win some ground for bettering the working lives has been seen throughout history. Despite the subversion, flouting and by-passing of laws, the right to a union acts like a safety valve, as we know from Mohan's account earlier in this chapter. A significant difference in the working conditions of garment and automobile workers can be attributed to greater levels of unionization in the latter. With the IR Code, the categories of workers who are eligible to be union members have reduced. Supervisors and apprentices are no longer considered workers and can no longer be union members. As a trade union organizer in Gurgaon remarked, 'The base of trade unions have shrunk with this law'.

There are restrictions imposed on which of the trade unions are qualified to negotiate with the managers. In an establishment with more than one registered union, the new code states that only the trade union having at least 51 per cent membership will be recognized as the negotiating union. However, since most industries have multiple registered trade unions, none of them may actually have the required membership and therefore qualify to be the negotiating union. Where earlier only trade unions in public utilities had to give prior notice before going on strike, now all unions have to do this. Once a strike has been declared illegal, supporters of the strike can be punished with a fine up to Rs 10,000 or a month's imprisonment. Another trade union organizer in Gurgaon remarked with anger and frustration, 'Legal strikes are not a possibility under this law'.

Companies which employed more than 100 workers had to earlier seek permission from the government prior to retrenching workers or declaring a lockout. This threshold has now been increased to 300 employees, thus exempting a large number of factories from this requirement. The legal category of Fixed Term Employment is a euphemism for contractual employment and the removal of a worker after the completion of her/his 'fixed term' will not be considered as retrenchment. Last but not least, labour inspectors will now be regarded as facilitators, and labour courts would be replaced by regional industrial tribunals and national industrial tribunals comprised of one judicial and one administrative member, thus rendering redressal of grievances even more difficult. A detailed note on the labour codes is included in Annexure I.

Conclusion

The Trade Union Act in 1926 codified the right to form a trade union. After Independence, the Constitution provided it the status of a fundamental right. We have travelled a long way since Independence. What began as instituting laws meant to broker peace and protect the worker has turned into anti-labour laws. Institutions such as courts have turned the right to protest into a 'law and order' problem. This attitude was clearly witnessed in the course of court hearings for Maruti workers, where it was stated that workers could not be granted bail since that would send a wrong signal to the investors. The early laws were premised on the imagination of tripartite settlements between a factory worker, factory owner and the state. The government has been, slowly but steadily, giving up all gestures of being a neutral arbitrator.

The factory worker, especially the one who enjoys some protection, has been relegated to history and replaced by unprotected, disposable workers. For others, it has meant that even the semblance of protection will be gone.

6. Looking Ahead

In 2021, as the second wave of the pandemic engulfed India, the surge in Covid-19 infections was accompanied by another surge – a surge in the number of billionaires in India. According to a list released by Forbes, in 2020, the total number of Indian billionaires rose from 102 to 140, and their combined wealth nearly doubled. India had the world's third highest number of billionaires, with 19 new additions in 2020 (TOI 2021). According to a report by the Johannesburg-based company New World Wealth, India was the second-most unequal country globally in 2016, with millionaires controlling more than half (54 per cent) of its wealth.[1] In 2020, even though the economy was shrinking, the bigger companies showed an increase in the share of profits and a fall in the share of wages they paid (Rajadhyaksha 2020). A rising tide does not lift all boats. The economy can grow, and the rich become richer without necessarily bettering the majority.

The reality of lives for most Indians is a desperate attempt to keep their heads above poverty or unfulfilled hopes of moving beyond their station of birth. Even today, most of our people are dependent

---

[1] In India, the richest 1 per cent own 53 per cent of the country's wealth, according to data from Credit Suisse. The richest 5 per cent own 68.6 per cent, while the top 10 per cent have 76.3 per cent. At the other end of the pyramid, the poorer 50 per cent jostle for a mere 4.1 per cent of national wealth. The data further shows that India's richest 1 per cent owned just 36.8 per cent of the country's wealth in 2000, while the share of the top 10 per cent was 65.9 per cent. Since then they have steadily increased their share of the pie. This is far ahead of the United States, where the richest 1 per cent own 37.3 per cent of total wealth. But India's richest still have a way to go before they match Russia, where the top 1 per cent own a stupendous 70.3 per cent of the country's wealth. See https://www.weforum.org/agenda/2016/10/inequality-in-india-oxfam-explainer Accessed on 10 April 2021.

on agriculture. The average incomes in this sector are meagre. Except for a few large farmers, most dependent on agriculture remain crushed under accumulated debt and despair. On the one hand, more and more people wish to move out of agriculture. On the other hand, those with small land holdings, who have migrated to the cities, are unwilling to let go of seemingly unviable pieces of land.[2] Though incomes in agriculture are meagre and there is limited scope for increasing those, even today, the land is the only social security for most people. Rations from the villages routinely supplement workers' wages in the garment industry. The villages house and feed the families of workers employed in the cities. The images of migrant workers flocking from the cities and factories back to the safety and security of their villages in 2020 and 2021 will not be forgotten in a hurry. Agriculture and the countryside are safe havens, but agriculture is unlikely to provide the income to uplift living standards significantly.

If not agriculture, then what? What are the options outside of agriculture? The service sector can provide high-paying jobs in financial or Information Technology (IT) services to a few people. Still, most people end up as delivery boys and girls for e-commerce giants. The conditions of work are brutal, and the wages dismal. Distributional inequality generated by e-commerce firms can be viewed in the example of Amazon. Jeffrey Bezos, founder of this multinational giant, made more in an hour in 2020 than one of his warehouse workers, would earn in a millennium (Gordon 2021). The template is the same in the United States of America or India.

Indeed, industry can provide jobs to migrant workers. Jobs in 'industry' include jobs in construction as well as manufacturing. Jobs in construction are seasonal and precarious in the extreme. These workers suffered considerable losses in work, livelihoods, and earnings because of the Covid-induced lockdown. The only

[2] As far back as in 2005, 40 per cent of the farmers were reported as wishing to quit agriculture, if they had a choice. – NSS as quoted by Perspectives, 'Harvesting Despair' (p. 161).

hope seems to lie in manufacturing then. A section of people who migrated from the villages to find work in the cities did find employment in the manufacturing sector.

In most cases, manufacturing jobs have also turned out to be much less desirable than imagined. This explains why Mohan does not want his children to work in virtually the 'best' segment of manufacturing – automobiles – in the country's capital. The overwhelming bulk of the workforce in the manufacturing sector in India is either employed in the unorganized sector or has informal work contracts such that bad quality jobs are a way of life. A manufacturing sector worker in India today is less likely to be a regular worker with fixed hours of work employed with Steel Authority of India Limited (SAIL) or Oil and Natural Gas Corporation Limited (ONGC) and more likely to be an overburdened, overworked, underpaid, casual worker tailoring garments or assembling phones for the global markets. In the globally integrated manufacturing segments, the pressure to remain competitive has forced downward pressure on wages. Competitiveness in the world market requires a country to lower its cost of production, and reducing the wage cost is an easy way to do this. World Bank has constructed the Ease of Doing Business (EoDB) index. A country with a higher score on the index is considered to be more competitive globally. A fall in the minimum wages and replacement of permanent jobs by Fixed Term Employment in any country improves its EoDB (Roychowdhury and Sarkar 2021:59).[3] In a period of merely five years, 2014-2019, India had jumped up 14 places to the 63rd position in the EoDB rankings (World Bank Group 2020).

How, then, can the standard of living be bettered for the vast majority? There is limited scope in agriculture, and the nature

---

[3] Ease of Doing Business Score ranges from 0 to 100 where 0 corresponds to worst performance. And 100 is the best. EoDB index improves if fixed term employment is offered in place of permanent jobs, minimum legal wages are removed, 'hire and fire' at will is allowed, weekly holidays and annual paid leave are suspended and an eight-hour workday is done away with.

of existing jobs in industry or services does not provide much hope either. One way forward is to bring the focus back to the manufacturing sector targeted to meet domestic demand. No sector other than manufacturing can provide the scope for an increase in productivity and wages and the possibility of absorbing people with different skill gradations. Standard, traditional manufacturing, like making cars or garments has the possibility of absorbing unskilled workers. And if the sector focuses on producing those goods which are demanded by large masses of people within the country, a way can be found where economic growth is associated with employment, ensuring decent livelihoods for the masses. When the pressure to become globally competitive is reduced, free-fall of wages can be prevented. Those employed in the factories will themselves generate demand for these goods, and the dependence on foreign demand can be reduced. Generating domestic demand for manufactured goods also requires a reduction in the inequality of incomes and wealth in the country. The demand has to come from the large majority of people who need to have the means to buy the goods. After all, how many cars or washing machines will the uber-rich buy? The bulk of demand will have to come from the masses, which can only happen if they are employed at decent wages. For example, factories can be set up which manufacture bicycles, inexpensive shirts, or consumer durables like televisions, less expensive phones, or other goods which are likely to be bought by workers employed in these factories. This can also be done in two-tier or three-tier cities of the country and thus ease the pressure of migration as well as move towards inter-regional equality. A rise in rural incomes and wages in the manufacturing sector could become the basis for mass demand for manufactured goods. A virtuous cycle can be created where the increase in wages fuels the demand for industrial goods, which in turn becomes the basis to produce more and consequently employ more people at decent wages.

For a country committed to bettering the lives and livelihoods of its people, the government also needs to step in to ensure adequate provision of basic necessities such as food, clothing, and shelter. To this basket of necessary goods should be added education and health. People can only spend on manufactured goods such as bicycles, mobile phones, or watches after their basic needs are satisfied. The importance and inadequacy of government spending on the health sector has been displayed during the Covid pandemic. Government health expenditure as a percentage of GDP for India fares poorly not just in comparison to richer countries such as China and Brazil but also to some poorer countries. For example, Kenya's per capita GDP is lower than India, but the Kenyan government still managed to spend roughly equivalent to 2.1 per cent of its GDP on healthcare in 2019 whereas the Indian government spent around 1 per cent of its GDP.[4] Even prior to the dire situation on account of Covid, in 2019, nearly one in five of the poorest households spent more on health than their annual per capita consumption expenditure (CSE 2019:76).

Manufacturing geared towards domestic demand must be premised on a tripartite settlement between workers, employers, and the government. The government must ensure that workers are provided basic social and legal protections. Pro-labour legislations founded on decades of workers' struggles must be restored and guaranteed. Laws providing social protection must be enacted and enforced. Minimum wages must become living wages. Living wages combined with safe and healthy working conditions will go a long way in creating a workforce that can move beyond the station of their birth. This will not only lead to economic betterment but also social stability. This requires a shift away from the understanding that commodifies and dehumanizes workers and allows markets to be the sole determinant of employment, wages and work conditions.

---

[4] Source of data: https://data.worldbank.org/indicator/SH.XPD.GHED. GD.ZS?most_recent_value_desc=false

Annexure I
Notes on Concepts and Legislations

1. GOOD AND BAD JOBS: NATURE OF EMPLOYMENT

We hear of regular and non-regular workers, formal and informal job contracts, and organized and unorganized sectors in India. Further, workers could be contract workers and casual workers. The organized and unorganized sectors are distinguished based on the size of the workforce and accompanying government regulations regarding working hours, hiring and firing norms, rights of association, minimum wages, and other aspects of employment. Formal and/or informal refers to the *nature of the employment* contract. As with the rest of the economy, the manufacturing sector is typically divided into organized and unorganized components. Organized manufacturing consists of those establishments that are large enough to be registered under the Factories Act (1947). These are typically establishments that employ ten or more workers with electricity or 20 or more workers without electricity, as per the official definition. The unorganized subsector was treated as the residual sector consisting of establishments that were not registered under the Factories Act. The related distinction between 'formal' and 'informal' employment (as opposed to enterprises) is used to distinguish between workers whose jobs are subject to labour regulation and who have access to job security versus those without such access.

The 17th International Conference of Labour Statisticians

defined informal employment as those jobs where '... employment relation is, in law or in practice, not subject to national labour legislation, income taxation, social protection or entitlement to certain employment benefits (advance notice of dismissal, severance pay, paid annual or sick leave, etc.' The unorganized sector largely has informal employment. Outside labour regulations, the organized sector is also witnessing the informalization of jobs and employment. India also has a large proportion of self-employed workers (50 per cent of total workers). Self-employed workers or those in 'own-account enterprises' also lie outside labour regulations and thus are part of informal workers.

What are good quality jobs? There is no fixed and unanimous definition of a good quality job. Different institutions provide different definitions, and what is considered 'good' would also vary across countries. The ILO would define a job as 'good' if it generates earnings that are sufficient to maintain a decent quality of life; provides security and social protection such that the risks of unemployment are limited and, in instances where the labourer is unable to obtain employment, they are able to fulfil basic needs through elements of social protection such as unemployment or pension benefits; ensures a safe and healthy work environment in which other non-wage aspects of employment, such as working relationships, are suitably desirable and finally enables labour to develop its capacities on the job, and partake of the fruits of technological advancement and more efficient production techniques (CSE 2018). Very few jobs and few workers in India would have 'good' jobs as per the above considerations.

National Commission on Enterprises in the Unorganised Sector (Sengupta et al. 2007) defined the unorganized sector (or informal sector) 'as all unincorporated private enterprises owned by individuals or households engaged in the sale and production of goods and services operated on a proprietary or partnership basis and with less than ten total workers'. The Commission identified informal workers as those 'working in the unorganized enterprises or households, excluding regular workers with social security benefits, and the workers in the formal sector without any employment and social security benefits provided by the employers'.

		Enterprise Type	Enterprise Type
		Organized	Unorganized
Employment Type	Formal	Regular salaried work with some job security and benefits, in enterprises employing ten or more workers*	Regular salaried employment with some benefits, in enterprises employing less than ten workers*
Employment Type	Informal	Various types of contract work and employment of short duration, without job security, in enterprises employing ten or more workers*	All types of casual work, work for daily, weekly, or monthly wages, and self-employment with no benefits or security, in enterprises employing less than ten workers*

Source: (CSE 2018: 94)

* Under the new labour codes, the threshold of 10 or more workers for organized enterprises will become 20 or more workers.

CSE (2018:96) develops three broad categories indicating the degree of formality and informality. The broadest definition is simply 'regular worker' (Formal 1). The second definition (Formal 2) is regular work with the availability of one of the following social security benefits: provident fund or pension, gratuity, healthcare/maternity benefits, or paid leave. The third and strictest definition (Formal 3) is the above plus a written contract.

The only nationally representative data sources going back in time are the periodic Employment-Unemployment Surveys of the NSSO (NSS-EUS). This survey has not been conducted since

2011-12. Since 2017, NSSO has begun to conduct the Periodic Labour Force Surveys (PLFS) to measure employment every three months in urban areas and once a year in both rural and urban areas. PLFS defines formal wage workers as wage workers having a written contract or receiving a social security benefit. Thus, formal workers can be defined as those with a written job contract or access to at least one social security benefit (provident fund/pension, gratuity, health care, maternity benefits). In 2015, only 17 per cent of the wage workers were 'formally' employed according to this definition. The share of the workforce with a written contract and some social security benefits was 10 per cent in manufacturing and 28 per cent in services.

Two other concepts in usage are that of regular and non-regular workers. According to the Seventh Central Pay Commission (CPC), a regular worker is defined as a person who has worked in non-farm enterprises and, in return, received a salary or wages on a regular basis (i.e., not based on the daily or periodic renewal of work contracts). This category includes not only persons getting time wage but also persons receiving piece wage or salary and paid apprentices, both full-time and part-time. Regular workers can be employed formally or informally. Regular wage workers accounted for 24 per cent of total employment in 2018-19, and less than half of those (around 41 per cent) fall into the formal regular wage workers category. A task force of the top economic policymaking body – the NITI Aayog, recommended that formal employment be redefined more 'pragmatically' to include workers covered under various provident funds, insurance, or pension schemes as well as workers subject to tax deduction at source (NITI Aayog 2017:16). This was suggested since written contracts are rare in India. This definition increases the size of the formal workforce to 15-25 per cent instead of the usually quoted figure of 7-10 per cent. These workers, around 10 per cent (9.7 per cent) of the workforce, have the highest average earnings. They draw a salary regularly and enjoy some social protection (Annexure-II, Table V). According to PLFS data, they comprised 12.9 per cent of the workforce in 2018-19, and the average monthly earnings for this category of workers was Rs 23,300 (see Annexure II, Table VI). The categories of contract and casual workers are explained below.

Contract Workers: A critical channel of informalization of work since the early 2000s, particularly in the manufacturing sector, has been the gradual replacement of workers directly employed by organized sector firms with workers hired via third-party contractors or 'contract workers'. These workers are generally not eligible for the range of benefits that direct workers receive. According to the Seventh CPC, contract workmen are indirect employees who are hired, supervised and remunerated by a contractor who, in turn, is compensated by the establishment.

Casual Workers: Towards the bottom of the hierarchy of employment contracts lie the casual workers. Casuals can be defined as workers who are employed as and when required and, as such, have no legal entitlement to the security of employment or leave and other benefits. The Seventh CPC defines a casual worker as a person, who is casually engaged in non-farm enterprises and, in return, receives wages according to the terms of the daily or periodic work contract. It can be said that casual employment is for a shorter term, less secure, and more irregular than temporary. Casual workers comprised 24.4 per cent of the workforce in 2018-19, and their average monthly earnings were estimated to be Rs 6,000 (CSE 2021: 49) (See Annexure II, Table VI).[1]

2. PREMATURE DEINDUSTRIALIZATION

The early developers of the world had experienced structural changes, which can be envisaged in terms of two interrelated processes – the Kuznets process (named after Simon Kuznets) and the Lewis process (named after Arthur Lewis). The first entails

---

[1] This analysis draws upon CSE 2018 (pp. 94-97) and CSE 2021 (pp. 47-49).

the movement of workers away from agriculture and related occupations to manufacturing and service activities. The second involves the linked movement of the workforce from micro and small-scale, informal, or unorganized economic activities where labour is underemployed to larger, formal or organized ones (SWI 2018:27). The late developers, especially countries of East Asia such as South Korea, Taiwan, Thailand, Malaysia, and China which developed after the Second World War shared one thing in common with the early developers and that is the role played by rapid industrialization in their development. The same is true for Japan after the nineteenth century. In what is often called the East Asian model, the government played an important role in stimulating the growth of industries in the private sector. One crucial difference between the development experiences of the two sets of countries is that compared to the early developers, similar shares of manufacturing in GDP were associated with much lower shares in employment in the case of East and Southeast Asia.

When we come to developing countries like India, we witness the phenomenon of premature deindustrialization – a situation wherein the growth of an economy's manufacturing sector begins to slow down prematurely in its path towards development. This means a shrinking proportion of the manufacturing sector in both output and employment. In other words, manufacturing reaches its peak share in output and employment at much lower levels of national income when compared to economies that underwent the transition earlier. Deindustrialization is not unique to India, and most of the advanced nations have also been deindustrialising, especially with respect to manufacturing industries' share of total employment. The share of employment generated by manufacturing has fallen for both United States and Britain, but for these countries, the contribution of manufacturing to GDP has not been affected as much. What is of concern in the case of India and some countries of Africa and Latin America is that these countries have experienced falling manufacturing shares in *both* employment and real value-added at much *lower* levels of national income when compared to the advanced economies. Many of these countries are turning into service economies without having gone through a proper experience of industrialization. In Latin America, as manufacturing has shrunk, informality has grown, and economy-wide productivity has suffered. In Africa, urban migrants are crowding into petty services instead of manufacturing. In the case of India, the share of services in total value-added has been increasing at the expense of industry. One explanation for premature deindustrialization in low- and middle-income countries is associated with globalization and the liberalization of trade. It is argued that large national increases in labour productivity have been counteracted by a shift of manufacturing jobs to lower productivity economies. Consequently, the average employment share in manufacturing that could be achieved has fallen over time, and countries have experienced deindustrialization earlier than they used to. The question which comes up very often is, can these countries have an alternative growth model and can the service sector act as the engine of growth for them?

3. POSSIBILITY OF SERVICE-LED GROWTH

Whether it was the early developers or the late developers, economic growth had been led by manufacturing during early stages of development. Services assumed leadership in economic growth only after the concerned country attained a certain level of per capita GDP. Indian experience stands out in contrast in this respect. India has thus far remained the rare lower-middle-income country to have experienced rapid services-led growth for several years. Economic Survey of 2013-14 noted that India's service sector exhibited the second fastest growth rate in the world (after China) from 2001 to 2012. According to C.P. Chandrasekhar and Jayati Ghosh, this trend has continued since. The share of services in GDP began to rise after the 1980s, and this was particularly sharp after 1996-97 (Chandrasekhar and Ghosh 2018). Today, more than half of India's GDP comes from the service sector. National Accounts Statistics (NAS), 2020, gave this figure as 53.6 per cent in 2018-19. (See Annexure II). Services have also been a significant contributor to India's exports. In 2016, the share of services in India's total exports (38 per cent) was much higher than in countries such as China, Mexico, and Brazil and close to ratios in the UK and the US. It has sometimes been argued that the service sector could be an engine of growth for India, and India's service-led growth could be seen as an example of a new twenty-first-century pattern of growth in low-income countries. On the face of it, the argument seems valid since services make up more than half of India's GDP, and the sector has been growing at a very fast rate. However, there are multiple problems with this argument:

(i) Divergence between contribution to output and contribution to employment: Although services form the major part of India's GDP, the sector has not been generating adequate employment. C.P. Chandrasekhar and Jayati Ghosh argue that India's experience has been unusual in one more respect: the wide divergence of the shares of the services sector in total gross value added and employment. The authors show that between 1999-00 and 2004-05, employment in the tertiary or the service sector increased by only 22 per cent, whereas GDP (at constant prices) contributed by the services sector expanded by 44 per cent. Tertiary sector employment in 2009-10 amounted to only 25 per cent of the workforce, even though around 55 per cent of GDP came from this sector. As compared to other countries, in 2015 and 2016, Gross Value Added (GVA) and employment shares of the service sector were 53 and 29 per cent in India (corresponding figures were 50 and 42 per cent in China, 60 and 61 per cent in Mexico, and 72 and 69 per cent in Brazil). The authors quote the Economic Survey 2016-17 to show that among the top 15 services producer countries, India had the lowest share of employment in the services sector as a proportion of total employment (28.6 per cent).

(ii) Composition of the service sector: The service sector comprises many different kinds of services. The NAS released by the Government of India shows that 'new', 'modern', and more productive services – transport, storage and communication, financial services, and real estate and professional services – *together* accounted for 27.4 per cent of GDP in 2012-13 and 28.6 per cent of GDP in 2019-20 (See Annexure II, Table VII).

These are the more skill-intensive services, and if these contribute around 25-30 per cent of GDP, it means that the remaining contribution of the service sector to India's GDP is made up of more traditional services such as the ones included in the category 'trade, repair, hotels and restaurants'. These traditional services are often unorganized, characterized by low earnings and represent a fall-back option for people with limited employment opportunities in the primary and secondary sectors. A report brought out by Azim Premji University categorized such activities as the 'surplus sector'. It showed that more than half of the employment generated by the service sector in 2016 was in the surplus sector.

The arguments above show that the service sector has failed to provide adequate employment. Also, employment lags far behind its contribution to output. Further, the sector is very heterogeneous where, on one hand, there is a low income, low productivity segment which provides high employment, such as petty retail trade or delivery work. On the other hand, there are modern services – real estate and professional services, which are high-income, but generate lower employment. This means that despite India's distinctive role in the rapid growth of services, the sector is unlikely to provide a route out of poverty.

4. FACTORY AND WORKSHOP

Both the terms are used as a description for physical spaces where manufacturing occurs. One distinction between the two is their evolution in history. Factories came into existence only in the last quarter of the eighteenth century. The production was mechanized or done with the help of machines; hence, one definition of the factory is – a building or group of buildings where goods are manufactured or assembled chiefly by machines. In contrast, the place of workshops in history preceded the industrial revolution, wherein manufacturing did take place but was more artisanal. In some ways, the factory aims at replication, while the workshop corresponds to customization. What is also important is how the factory is defined legally since that provides the ambit for applicability of the laws. In India, the Factories Act of 1948 defined a factory as the 'premises or precincts' wherein ten or more workers carry on manufacturing with the aid of power, or 20 or more workers carry on manufacturing without the aid of power. This threshold has been doubled under the new labour codes. To be classified as a factory under the OSHWC Code, a unit now has to employ twenty personnel if it uses power, and forty personnel without power. The proviso to the definition states that where any law in force in a State specifies a threshold more or less than that specified above, the same shall prevail until it is amended by the competent legislature.

5. MINIMUM WAGE, LIVING WAGE, FAIR WAGE

India passed the Minimum Wages Act in 1948 to ensure a minimum level of wage protection for workers. According to the Ministry of Labour and Employment, a tripartite 'Committee on Fair Wage', was set up in 1948 to provide guidelines for wage structures in the country. The report of this Committee was a significant landmark in the history of the formulation of wage policy in India. Its recommendations set out the key concepts of the 'living wage', 'minimum wages', and 'fair wage' besides setting out guidelines for wage fixation. Defining the concept of minimum wage, The Committee on Fair Wage states that 'the *minimum wage* must provide not only for the bare sustenance of life but for the preservation of the efficiency of the workers. For this purpose, minimum wage must provide some measures of education, medical requirements and amenities. In further elucidation of the concept of minimum wage, the Supreme Court has repeatedly stated that minimum wages should be determined by need-based criteria that extend beyond basic physical needs. As far back as 1992, in a landmark ruling Supreme Court said that the need-based criteria should include specific nutrition requirements (defined in calories), clothing and housing needs, medical expenses, family expenses, education, fuel, lighting, festival expenses, provisions for old age and other miscellaneous expenditure. (Workmen Represented by Secretary vs. Management of Reptakos Brett)

Labour law in India is a concurrent subject, meaning it comes under the jurisdiction of both central and state governments. The 'appropriate government' fixes and revises the minimum wage. The central government is responsible for some specified types of employment. In all other areas of employment, it is the respective state government that establishes the minimum wage. The wage rate may be fixed on a daily, hourly, or even monthly basis. The 1948 Act provides for review and revision of minimum wages every five years, if not earlier. According to Section 3(1)(b), the 'appropriate government' may review at such intervals as it may deem fit, such intervals not exceeding five years, and revise the minimum rate of wages, if necessary. To have a uniform wage structure and to reduce the disparity in minimum wages across the country, the concept of the National Floor Level Minimum Wage was mooted based on the recommendations of the National Commission on Rural Labour (NCRL) in 1991. Keeping in view the recommendation of NCRL and subsequent rises in price indices, the National Floor Level Minimum

Wage was fixed at Rs 35 per day in 1996. This is a non-statutory measure, and the state governments are persuaded to fix minimum wages such that the minimum wage is not less than the National Floor Level Minimum Wage in any scheduled employments.

A *living wage* is the lowest wage at which the wage earner and their family can afford the most basic cost of living. The term living wage ensures a basic standard of living, which includes good health, dignity, comfort, and education. It also provides for contingencies. Although living wage and minimum wage are often used interchangeably, the minimum wage is mandated and enforced by legislation, whereas a living wage is not. The demand for an increase in minimum wage often intersects with the need to earn a living wage. A living wage is fixed considering the general economic conditions of the country. The concept of a *fair wage* is essentially linked with the capacity of the industry to pay. The lower limit of the fair wage is the minimum wage; the upper limit is set by the capacity of the industry to pay. Fair wages, thus, depend on considerations such as the condition of the industry, the productivity of labour, and so on.

6. NEW LABOUR CODES

Described by the government as the 'biggest labour reforms in Independent India', the four labour codes introduced by the Ministry of Labour and Employment have replaced 29 of the 44 labour laws that existed before 2019. Although the codes were supposed to be implemented from 1 April 2021, they are yet to be implemented as the central government and state governments are in the process of drafting rules for them. The following table lists the labour laws that have been repealed and subsumed by the four labour codes: (1) Code on Wages, 2019; Industrial Relations Code, 2020; (3) Occupational Safety, Health and Working Conditions (OSHWC) Code, 2020; and (4) Code on Social Security, 2020.

Labour Codes	Legislations that have been repealed and subsumed
Code on Wages, 2019	Payment of Wages Act, 1936; Minimum Wages Act, 1948; Payment of Bonus Act, 1965; and Equal Remuneration Act, 1976
Industrial Relations Code, 2020	Trade Unions Act, 1926; Industrial Employment (Standing Orders) Act, 1946, and Industrial Disputes Act, 1947
Occupational Safety, Health and Working Conditions Code, 2020	Factories Act, 1948; Mines Act, 1952; Dock Workers (Safety, Health and Welfare) Act, 1986; Building and Other Construction Workers (Regulation of Employment and Conditions of Service) Act, 1996; Plantations Labour Act, 1951; Contract Labour (Regulation and Abolition) Act, 1970; Inter-State Migrant Workmen (Regulation of Employment and Conditions of Service) Act, 1979; Working Journalist and other Newspaper Employees (Conditions of Service and Miscellaneous Provision) Act, 1955; Working Journalist (Fixation of Rates of Wages) Act, 1958; Motor Transport Workers Act, 1961; Sales Promotion Employees (Condition of Service) Act, 1976; Beedi and Cigar Workers (Conditions of Employment) Act, 1966; and Cine-Workers and Cinema Theatre Workers (Regulation of Employment) Act, 1981
Code on Social Security, 2020	Employees' Provident Funds and Miscellaneous Provisions Act, 1952; Employees' State Insurance Act, 1948; Employees' Compensation Act, 1923; Employment Exchanges (Compulsory Notification of Vacancies) Act, 1959; Maternity Benefit Act, 1961; Payment of Gratuity Act, 1972; Cine-workers Welfare Fund Act, 1981; Building and Other Construction Workers' Welfare Cess Act, 1996; and Unorganised Workers Social Security Act, 2008

Source: https://prsindia.org/billtrack/overview-of-labour-law-reforms

Why the labour codes may take away key safeguards and increase insecurity for industrial workers

(i) Diluting the criterion for determining minimum wages

The Code on Wages has done away with established criteria for determining minimum wages. It gives considerable discretionary powers to the 'the appropriate government' i.e., the executive authorities at the site, to 'take into account the skill required, the arduousness of the work, geographical location of the place of work and other factors as may be prescribed' to determine wages (PUDR 2021:17). The code states that the central government will declare a floor wage at the national level and state governments cannot declare a minimum wage *below* this (see Section 9). No specific criteria are laid out to determine the floor wages. This has already resulted in divergence between the minimum wage and the national floor wage. A government-appointed committee in 2018 (Anoop Satpathy Committee) recommended a minimum wage of Rs 375 per day, whereas the national floor wage declared in the same year was Rs 176 per day. This is likely to adversely impact the minimum wages set by different states since they are supposed to take the national floor wage as the *floor* and minimum wages may slide downwards.

(ii) More establishments exempted from paying bonus

The provision of exemption of new establishments from paying bonus (already there in the Payment of Bonus Act, 1965), has been further expanded in the Code on Wages, 2019, 'using an ambiguous language for defining new establishments'. The code further 'undermines transparency by prohibiting authorities from disclosing balance sheets without the express permission of the employer' (see Section 31) (PUDR 2021:19).

(iii) Possibility of overtime work without overtime payment

The Code on Wages 'opens the door to compulsory overtime without extra payment' by removing a clear definition of overtime and allowing complementary and intermittent work to exceed normal hours (see Section 13) (PUDR 2021:19).

(iv) Reducing the categories of employees who are eligible to become trade union members

The Industrial Relations Code, 2020 has brought in major changes which will impact the base of trade unions and the ability of workers to organise. The category of workers itself has been shrunk which used to be the basis of forming a trade union. Section 2 (zr, iv) of the code excludes supervisors earning more than Rs 18,000 per month from the category of workers. 'Apprentices' are also excluded from the category of workers. With growing proportion of trainees and apprentices, this is likely to shrink the base of formation of a trade union.

(v) Legitimising contractual employment as Fixed Term Employment

This change will have serious repercussions for permanent jobs. After the completion of fixed term, removal of workers will not be considered as retrenchment. This would encourage the 'hire and fire' policy and increase job precarity. According to the report by PUDR, 'this form reinforces employers' power as renewal of employment is entirely in the hands of the management' (PUDR 2021: 22).

(vi) Curtailing the right to organise

The right to organise included in the now-repealed Industrial Disputes Act (IDA) has been seriously compromised by the Industrial Relations Code. In order to be recognised as the Single Negotiating Union in the enterprise, the code stipulates that the union must have membership of at least 51 per cent of the workers. If there is no union which fulfils this criterion, then a Negotiating Council can be formed but only those unions can send representatives in this council who have at least 20 per cent workers as its members. According to the PUDR report, 'It is a fact that in most of the industries where multiple registered trade unions are working none of them will have 51% membership, thus they lose their recognition from the management even if one of them has a majority, i.e., even if 49% of the workers support one union' (PUDR 2021: 22).

(vii) Curtailing the right to strike

The IR Code stipulates that no establishment can go on strike without giving notice prior to the date of actual strike. Till now, a prior notice used to be essential only in the case of public utilities. The period of prior notice is also not clear, as it is simultaneously mentioned as 60 days and 14 days in the legislation (Chapter VIII, Section 62 of the IR Code). Once notice is served, a labour administrator is supposed to initiate the conciliation process within the notice period; during the process of conciliation and arbitration, trade unions are legally bound not to go on strike. Further, mass casual leave involving at least 50 per cent of workers is construed as a strike. Once a strike has been declared illegal, supporters of the strike can be slapped with financial penalty and even face imprisonment.

(viii) Exemptions for retrenching workers and declaring lockouts

The provisions of the IR Code are applicable to industrial establishments which have at least 300 workers (Chapter X, Section 77(1)). By implication, factories and enterprises employing less than 300 workers will not require government permission for retrenching workers or for declaring a lockout. This exemption used to be enjoyed earlier by firms with less than

100 workers. According to the PUDR report, 'If the government does not respond within 60 days for permission for closure, lay-offs and retrenchment, it will be taken that permission has been granted. The government can thus render appeals and challenges by workers futile, simply through inaction' (PUDR 2021: 23).

(ix) Dismantling labour courts and quasi-judicial institutions for labour grievances

The Industrial Disputes Act provided for Courts of Enquiry, Labour Courts, Industrial Tribunals and National Industrial Tribunals. Under the IR Code 2020, there will be no labour courts. Industrial tribunals would exist, both at the national level and the regional level. Earlier these tribunals and labour courts had only judicial officers; now administrative officers and members of the executive can also be made members.

(x) Removing the applicability of safety and working conditions code for smaller enterprises

The OSHWC Code has changed the threshold of applicability of safeguards relating to occupational safety, health and working conditions of workers. Earlier, any manufacturing unit employing ten or more workers (with the use of electric power) and twenty or more workers (without the use of electric power) was classified as a factory. OSHWC Code has doubled this threshold, implying that a section of workers who had been protected by various labour laws applicable to factories previously, will no longer be so. Earlier, factories employing 100 or more workers were supposed to be supervised under 'safety committees'. Now, this will be applicable only for factories employing 500 or more workers and 250 or more workers in case of dangerous operations. 'With the argument that smaller units need to be encouraged by reducing the burden of compliance, workers in smaller establishments are thus not covered by safety and welfare measures. This is particularly pertinent given that nearly 80 per cent of Indian workers are employed in small economic units and a vast workforce will now not be entitled to safe workplaces' (PUDR 2021: 27).

(xi) Diluting safety norms

Safety norms have been diluted in other ways as well. The now-repealed Factories Act, 1948 mentioned the maximum permissible limits of exposure to chemical and toxic substances in various manufacturing processes. OSHWC is silent on these upper limits. Safety norms for women workers have also been diluted. Until now, women could not be forced to work between 7 pm and 6 am. This has been relaxed now. Further, scope for women workers to be employed in risky work has been opened.

(xii) Removing limits on overtime work

The Factories Act, 1948 had put a maximum limit to overtime (OT) hours. The maximum overtime was 12 hours per week and 50 hours for a period of three months. Section 27 of OSHWC does not specify maximum hours of OT. This has been left to the concerned governments.

(xiii) Exempting more establishments from contract labour regulations

The Contract Labour Act of 1970 had spelt out some stipulations which had to be followed by establishments and contractors employing twenty or more contract workers. This threshold has also been raised to 50 workers (Chapter XI, Part I, Section 45) implying that firms with 49 contract workers will remain outside the purview of regulations. Firms employing five workers or more were required to submit a list of migrant workers employed by it, to the labour department. As part of OSHWC Code, this has been raised to firms with ten or more workers (Chapter XI, Part II, Section 59).

(xiv) Holding the worker responsible for industrial accidents

According to the PUDR report, 'another important and very dangerous provision in OSHWC Code 2020 is that it makes a worker accountable for industrial accidents along with the management – if a worker is found to be responsible for any accident he/she will be fined upto Rs 10,000 and imprisonment' (PUDR 2021: 30) (see section 106 read with section 13 of the OSHWC Code).

(xv) Ambiguity regarding financing and implementation of social security coverage for unorganised sector workers

The Social Security Code, 2020, has broadened the definition of unorganised sector workers to include home-based workers, self-employed, gig and platform workers. A welcome step, but ambiguity remains on how this would be financed or extended in practice.

(xvi) Option for owners, workers and employers to opt out of the Employees Provident Fund Scheme (EPF) and the Employees' State Insurance Corporation (ESIC)

The proviso to Section 1(5) of the Social Security Code, 2020 says that if the owners, workers and employees of any firm (by majority) wish to opt out of EPF scheme, they can do so. Similarly, the proviso to section 1(7) of the Code stipulates that the employers and employees of any firm (by majority) can also opt out of the ESIC scheme.

(xvii) Reducing the contribution of employers and employees towards ESIC

The ESIC contribution rates for employers and employees have been reduced from 4.75 and 1.75 per cent respectively to 3.25 and 0.75 per cent respectively (Source: Official website of Ministry of Labour and Employment, Government of India https://labour.gov.in/general-overview).

Select sections from Code on Wages, 2019

Section 9 (1) The Central Government shall fix floor wage taking into account minimum living standards of a worker in such manner as may be prescribed:

Provided that different floor wage may be fixed for different geographical areas.

(2) The minimum rates of wages fixed by the appropriate government under section 6 shall not be less than the floor wage and if the minimum rates of wages fixed by the appropriate Government earlier is more than the floor wage, then, the appropriate Government shall not reduce such minimum rates of wages fixed by it earlier.

Section 13 (1) Where the minimum rates of wages have been fixed under this Code, the appropriate Government may – (a) fix the number of hours of work which shall constitute a normal working day inclusive of one or more specified intervals; (b) provide for a day of rest in every period of seven days which shall be allowed to all employees or to any specified class of employees and for the payment of remuneration in respect of such days of rest; (c) provide for payment for work on a day of rest at a rate not less than the overtime rate.

(2) The provisions of sub-section (1) shall, in relation to the following classes of employees apply, only to such extent and subject to such conditions as may be prescribed, namely:–

(a) employees engaged in any emergency which could not have been foreseen or prevented; (b) employees engaged in work of the nature of preparatory or complementary work which must necessarily be carried on outside the limits laid down for the general working in the employment concerned;

(c) employees whose employment is essentially intermittent;

(d) employees engaged in any work which for technical reasons has to be completed before the duty is over; and

(e) employees engaged in a work which could not be carried on except at times dependent on the irregular action of natural forces.

(3) For the purposes of clause (c) of sub-section (2), employment of an employee is essentially intermittent when it is declared to be so by the appropriate Government on the ground that the daily hours of duty of the employee, or if there be no daily hours of duty as such for the employee, the hours of duty normally include periods of inaction during which the employee may be on duty but is not called upon to display either physical activity or sustained attention.

Section 31 (1) The bonus shall be paid out of the allocable surplus which shall be an amount equal to sixty per cent in case of a banking company and sixty-seven per cent in case of other establishment, of the available surplus and the available surplus shall be the amount calculated in accordance with section 33.

(2) Audited accounts of companies shall not normally be questioned.

(3) Where there is any dispute regarding the quantum of bonus, the authority notified by the appropriate Government having jurisdiction may call upon the employer to produce the balance sheet before it, but the authority shall not disclose any information contained in the balance sheet unless agreed to by the employer.

Select sections from Industrial Relations Code, 2020

Section 2 (o): 'Fixed term employment' means the engagement of a worker on the basis of a written contract of employment for a fixed period: Provided that –

(a) his hours of work, wages, allowances and other benefits shall not be less than that of a permanent worker doing the same work or work of similar nature;

(b) he shall be eligible for all statutory benefits available to a permanent worker proportionately according to the period of service rendered by him even if his period of employment does not extend to the qualifying period of employment required in the statute; and

(c) he shall be eligible for gratuity if he renders service under the contract for a period of one year

Section 86(13): Any worker who commences, continues or otherwise acts in furtherance of a strike which is illegal under this Code, shall be punishable with fine which shall not be less than one thousand rupees, but which may extend up to ten thousand rupees or with imprisonment for a term which may extend to one month, or with both.

Select sections from the Occupational Safety, Health and Working Conditions Code, 2020

Section 27: There shall be paid wages at the rate of twice the rate of wages in respect of overtime work, where a worker works in an establishment or class of establishment for more than such hours of work in any day or in any week as may be prescribed by the appropriate Government and the period of overtime work shall be calculated on a daily basis or weekly basis, whichever is more favourable to such worker.

13. Every employee at workplace shall, –

(a) take reasonable care for the health and safety of himself and of other persons who may be affected by his acts or omissions at the workplace;

(b) comply with the safety and health requirements specified in the standards;

(c) co-operate with the employer in meeting the statutory obligations of the employer under this Code;

(d) if any situation which is unsafe or unhealthy comes to his attention, as soon as practicable, report such situation to his employer or to the health and safety representative and in case of mine, agent or manager referred to in section 67, safety officers or an official for his workplace or section thereof, as the case may be, who shall report it to the employer in the manner as may be prescribed by the appropriate Government;

(e) not wilfully interfere with or misuse or neglect any appliance, convenience or other thing provided at workplace for the purpose of securing the health, safety and welfare of workers;

(f) not do, wilfully and without reasonable cause, anything, likely to endanger himself or others; and

(g) perform such other duties as may be prescribed by the appropriate Government.

106. (1) Subject to the provisions of section 13, except clause (d) thereof, if any employee employed in a workplace contravenes any provision of this Code or any rules or orders made thereunder, imposing any duty or liability on employee, he shall be punishable with penalty which may extend to ten thousand rupees.

Social Security Code, 2020

Proviso to Section 1(5): Provided that where the employer of an establishment to which the provisions of Chapter III (Employee Provident Fund) applied under this sub-section desires to come out of such applicability, he may make an application to the Central Provident Fund Commissioner and the Central Provident Fund Commissioner shall, if satisfied that there is an agreement between the employer and majority of the employees to this effect, *make the provisions of that Chapter inapplicable* to such establishment, in such manner and subject to such conditions as may be prescribed by the Central Government (emphasis added).

Proviso to Section 1(7): Provided that where the employer of an establishment to which the provisions of Chapter IV (Employees

State Insurance Corporation) applied under this sub-section *desires to come out of such applicability*, he may make an application to the Director General of the Corporation and Director General of the Corporation shall, if satisfied that there is an agreement between the employer and majority of the employees to this effect, make the provisions of that Chapter inapplicable to such establishment, in such manner and subject to such conditions as may be prescribed by the Central Government (emphasis added).

7. TEXT OF THE GOOD CONDUCT BOND ISSUED TO MSIL WORKERS, MANESAR, JUNE 2011

In Terms of Clause 25 (3) of the Certified Standing Orders, I (worker's name), son of ……, do hereby execute and sign this good conduct bond voluntarily in my own volition in accordance with Clause 25 (3) of the Certified Standing Orders. I undertake that upon joining my duties I shall give normal production in disciplined manner and that I shall not resort to go slow, intermittent stoppage of work, stay-in strike, work to rule, sabotage or otherwise indulge in any activity, which would hamper the normal production in the factory. I am aware that resorting to go slow, intermittent stoppage of work, stay-in strike, or indulging in any other activity having adverse effect on the normal production constitutes a major misconduct under the Certified Standing Orders and the punishment provided for committing such acts of misconducts includes dismissal from service without notice, under clause 30 of the Certified Standing Orders.

I, therefore, do hereby agree that if, upon joining my duties, I am found indulging in any activity such as go slow, intermittent stoppage of work, stay-in strike, work to rule, sabotage or any other activity, having the effect of hampering normal production, I shall be liable to be dismissed from service as provided under the Certified Standing Orders.

I agree that if on joining duty I am found indulging in go slow, intermittent stoppage of work, stay-in strike, work to rule, sabotage or otherwise indulge in any activity, which would hamper the normal production in the factory, I will be liable to be dismissed from service without notice, as provided under the Certified Standing Orders.

i) Apply or obtain leave on false pretext

ii) Lack of proper personal appearance, sanitation and cleanliness including proper grooming

iii) Conduct in private life prejudicial to the reputation of the company

iv) Remaining in a toilet for a substantially long period of time

v) Habitual neglect of cleanliness

Date

Signature of the workman

(Quoted by Barnes 2018: 115)

Annexure II
Facts and Figures

I. SHARE OF AGRICULTURE, INDUSTRY AND SERVICES IN OUTPUT AND EMPLOYMENT

Note: Industry includes both manufacturing and construction

a) Share in GDP (%)

Years	Agriculture	Industry	Services
2009	16.74	31.12	45.98
2010	17.03	30.73	45.03
2011	17.19	30.16	45.44
2012	16.85	29.4	46.3
2013	17.15	28.4	47.27
2014	16.79	27.66	47.82
2015	16.17	27.35	47.78
2016	16.36	26.62	47.75
2017	16.36	26.48	48.89
2018	15.41	26.13	48.81
2019	15.96	24.88	48.88

b) Share in workforce (%)

Years	Agriculture	Industry	Services
2010	51.52	21.81	26.68
2011	48.98	23.49	27.53
2012	47	24.36	28.64

2013	46.36	24.55	29.09
2014	45.84	24.55	29.61
2015	45.67	24.06	30.27
2016	45.14	23.98	30.87
2017	44.05	24.7	31.25
2018	43.33	24.95	31.72
2019	42.39	25.5	32.04
2020	41.49	26.18	32.33

Source: Statista

Traditionally, the economic activities of an economy are divided into the primary sector, which largely comprises extractive activities such as agriculture; the secondary sector or industry, which has transformative activities and includes both manufacturing and construction and finally, the tertiary or the service sector.

The actual figures depend on the sources used. On account of changes in methodologies, it is difficult to find one consistent source for the contribution of different sectors to income and employment over the years. However, the tables given in the earlier note and the one given below show broad trends over different decades.

II. OUTPUT AND EMPLOYMENT BY ECONOMIC ACTIVITY (%)

		1977 -78	1982 -83	1987 -88	1993 -94	1999 -00	2004 -05	2009 -10	2011 -12
AGR	Output	40.39	37.31	32.96	31.50	26.30	21.89	16.94	16.48
	Employment	71.48	68.89	65.53	64.69	60.95	57.08	52.42	47.49
MFG	Output	22.84	22.79	23.71	23.47	23.85	25.06	25.98	26.11
	Employment	12.16	13.17	15.20	14.24	15.67	18.15	21.25	23.53
TRD	Output	15.85	17.27	18.14	18.04	21.19	24.49	26.53	26.72

	Em-ployment	8.18	8.78	9.78	10.45	13.95	14.89	15.71	16.49
CSP	Output	20.93	22.64	25.19	26.99	28.66	28.56	30.56	30.70
	Em-ployment	8.11	8.81	9.31	10.63	9.57	9.91	10.55	12.49

Source: Calculations done by author based on Basu and Das (2015) with output calculations in the table cited based on 2004-05 prices.

Note: AGR =Agriculture, forestry, mining and allied activities

MFG = Manufacturing, construction, electricity, gas and water supply

TRD = Trade, transport and communication

CSP = Community, social and personal services

III. SECTORAL EMPLOYMENT SHARES FOR INDIA

Sector	2011	2018
Agriculture	47.00	41.39
Construction	10.74	12.24
Manufacturing	12.48	12.13
Mining	0.58	0.43
Services	28.64	33.24
Utilities	0.55	0.58

Source: Table 3 in Basole (2022: 26).

IV. CONTRIBUTION (PERCENTAGE OF OUTPUT) OF AGRICULTURE, MANUFACTURING AND SERVICES TO GROSS VALUE ADDED AT BASIC PRICES (OUTPUT AT 2011-12 PRICES)

Years	Agriculture	Manufacturing	Services
2016-17	15.2	18.1	53.2
2017-18	15.1	18.1	52.7
2018-19	14.6	18.0	53.6

Source: Calculated from National Accounts Statistics 2020

V. SHARES OF DIFFERENT CATEGORIES OF WORKERS IN 2018-19 (%)

Employment type (UPSS)	Urban	Total
Formal regular wage worker	21.7	9.7
Informal regular wage worker	27	14.1
Regular wage worker (1+2)	48.7	23.8
Own account worker	28.8	36.6
Employer	3.8	2.3
Unpaid family worker	5.2	13.2
Self-employed (4+5+6)	37.8	52.0
Casual/daily wage worker	13.5	24.2
Total (3+7 +8)	100	100
Share of informal workers in total (9-1)	78.3	90.3

Source: (CSE 2021: 47)

VI. SHARE IN THE WORKFORCE AND MONTHLY EARNINGS BY CATEGORY OF WORKERS (2018-19)

Category of Worker	Share in work-force (%)	Monthly Earnings (Rs)
Formal Regular	12.9	23,300
Informal Regular	11.6	9300
Self-Employed	51.0	11000
Casual/Daily wage worker	24.4	6000

Note: Monthly earning for casual worker = Daily earning multiplied by 26

Source: (CSE 2021: 49)

VII. PERCENTAGE CHANGE IN GVA BY ECONOMIC ACTIVITY (2011-12 PRICES)

	2012 -13	2013 -14	2014 -15	2015 -16	2016 -17	2017 -18	2018 -19	2019 -20
1. Agriculture, forestry, fishing	1.5	5.6	-0.2	0.6	6.8	6.6	2.6	4.3
3. Manufacturing	5.5	5.0	7.9	13.1	7.9	7.5	5.3	-2.4
5. Construction	0.3	2.7	4.3	3.6	5.9	5.2	6.3	1.0
6. Trade, repair, hotels, restaurants	11.1	5.4	9.8	11.1	10.1	12.9	8.8	7.1
7. Transport, storage, communication & services related to broadcasting	7.6	8.4	8.8	8.9	3.5	5.7	3.8	5.0
8. Financial services	10.3	9.1	8.5	7.3	3.4	4.7	4.7	4.1
9. Real Estate, Ownership of Dwellings, Professional Services	9.5	12.1	12.2	12.1	10.8	0.6	8.1	8.5
Public administration, defence	2.1	1.7	6.6	3.9	8.7	10.1	6.8	7.2
Other services	6.3	5.7	9.7	8.0	9.8	6.9	7.9	9.2

TOTAL GVA at basic prices	5.4	6.1	7.2	8.0	8.0	6.2	5.9	4.1

Source: From Statement 1.6 B, NAS 2021

Note: The table excludes categories Mining (S. No. 2) and Electricity, Gas, Water Supply and other utilities (S. No. 4).

VIII. MINIMUM WAGE IN HARYANA W.E.F JULY 1, 2019

Category	Minimum Wage	Daily Wage
Unskilled	8827.40	347.08
Semi-skilled A	9268.75	364.43
Semi-skilled B	9732.18	382.66
Skilled A	10,218.79	401.79
Skilled B	10,729.74	421.88
Highly Skilled	11,266.23	442.97

Source: http://www.labourlaw.co.in/minimum-wages-haryana-010119/ minimum-wages-haryana-010119.html .

Definitions of categories

(i) Unskilled: An unskilled employee is one who does operations that involve the performance of simple duties, which require the experience of little or no independent judgment or previous experience, although familiarity with the occupational environment is necessary. His work may thus require, in addition to physical exertion, familiarity with a variety of articles or goods.

(ii) Semi-skilled: A semi-skilled worker is one who does work generally of defined routine nature wherein the major requirement is not so much of the judgment or skill but for the proper discharge of duties assigned to him or a relatively narrow job and where others make important decisions. His work is thus limited to performing routine operations of limited scope.

(iii) Skilled: A skilled employee is one who is capable of working efficiently, exercising considerable independent judgement, and discharging his duties with responsibility. He must possess a thorough knowledge of the trade, craft or industry in which he is employed.

(iv) Highly Skilled: A highly skilled worker can work efficiently and supervise skilled employees' work.

Wages per month are calculated as 4.33 times if a weekly wage is defined. It is calculated as 4.33 times the standard weekly hours if an hourly wage is given.

IX. BASIC PAY FOR A SAMPLER OR A SAMPLING TAILOR FROM 2007-2015

Years	Basic Pay (monthly) (Rs) (Nominal terms)	Rate of Growth (money / nominal wages)	Price Index (CPI(IW)) Base: 2001=100	Salary adjusted for price change (Basic salary in real terms)	Rate of Growth (real wages)
2007	3900		131	2977.09	
2008	3976	.019 (1.9%)	141.6	2819.85	5.2%
2009	4304	.082 (8.2%)	157	2741.4	-2.7%
2010	4739	.10 (10%)	175.9	2708	-1.2%
2011	5031	.061 (6.1%)	191.5	2634	-2.7%
2012	5400	.073 (7.3%)	209.3	2583.7	-1.9%
2013	5600	.037 (3.7%)	232.16	2413.7	-6.5%
2014	6030	.076 (7.6%)	246.9	2451.2	1.5%
2015	6200	.028 (2.8%)	261.4	2371.8	-3.2%

Note: CPI(IW) is the consumer price index for industrial workers. Base 2001=100 means that prices if (of basket of goods normally purchased by industrial workers) in 2001 are treated as 100, then the index in subsequent years shows the change in prices relative to 2001. Hence an index of 131 in 2007 means that relative to 2001, these prices have risen by 31 per cent. The rise in CPI(IW) is the measure of inflation relevant for industrial workers.

Source: Labour Bureau, Ministry of Labour and Employment, GoI for CPI (IW) and interviews with garment workers for data on monthly basic pay.

Bibliography

Aggarwal, Archana. 2012. 'India's Service Sector Gateway to Development'. *Economic and Political Weekly*, June 30, 2012. Vol XLVII, Nos 26 & 27: 119-123.

Amit and Nayanjyoti. 2018. 'Changes in production and labour regimes and challenges before collective bargaining: A study focusing on the Gurgaon-Neemrana Industrial Belt in the DMIC', State of Working India, Background Paper 18. Centre for Sustainable Employment, Azim Premji University. Accessed from https://cse.azimpremjiuniversity.edu.in/state-of-workingindia/ on 04-04-2023

Barnes, Tom. 2018. *Making Cars in the New India: Industry, Precarity and Informality*. Cambridge University Press.

Basole, Amit. 2022. 'Structural Transformation and Employment Generation In India: Past Performance and the Way Forward'. *Keynote Paper at ISLE Conference*, April 11, 2022.

Basu, Deepankar and Debarshi Das. (2015). 'Employment Elasticity in India and the US, 1977-2011: A Sectoral Decomposition Analysis'. Working Paper Number 2015-07, Economics Department Working Paper Series, University of Massachusetts, Amherst.

Beaud, Michel. 1983/2004. *A History of Capitalism 1500-2000*. Monthly Review Press/Aakar Books for South Asia.

Braverman, Harry. 1974/2006. *Labour And Monopoly Capital: The Degradation of Work in the Twentieth Century*. Monthly Review Press/Cornerstone Publications.

Centre for Sustainable Employment. 2018. *State of Working India*. Azim Premji University.

Centre for Sustainable Employment. 2019. *State of Working India*.

Azim Premji University.

Centre for Sustainable Employment. 2021. *State of Working India*. Azim Premji University.

Chakraborty, Amit and Praveen Jha. 2012. 'Emerging Dynamics of Global Production Networks and Labour Process: A Study from India'. Paper in International Workshop on 'New Spatialities and Labour', 6-8 July 2012, IGIDR, Mumbai.

Chhabra, Ronak. 2020 'Honda Protest and How it Ended: A Sneak Peek into Dismal Labour Practices in India'. Newsclick. 7 March.

Dewey, Clive. 1993. *Anglo-Indian Attitudes: Mind of the Indian Civil Service*. Bloomsbury.

Government of NCT of Delhi (GNCTD). 2021. Economic Survey of Delhi 2019-2020. http://delhiplanning.nic.in/content/ economic-survey-delhi-2019-20

GoI, Ministry of Commerce and Industry. 'Brief about Industrial Policy'. https://dipp.gov.in/policies-rules-and-acts/policies/ industrial-policy . Brief about Industrial Policy (viewed on 15 April 2021)

Gordon, Colin. 2021. 'Amazon doesn't know how to innovate. It knows how to exploit'. *Jacobin Magazine*. 19 April 2021.

Goyal, Malini. 2019. 'With India's economy growing at about 7 per cent, why the auto industry is hurting so badly?' *The Economic Times*. 28 April.

Himanshu. 2020. 'India: extreme inequality in numbers'. *Oxfam International Report*. https://www.oxfam.org/en/india- extreme-inequality-number .

Hope, Katie. 2017. 'Has this dress been to more countries than you?' BBC News, March 22. https://www.bbc.com/news/ business-39337204 .

Khera, Reetika and Meghna Yadav. 2020. 'What pay ratios in NIFTY50 companies tell us about income inequality in India'. Accessed from https://www.ideasforindia.in/topics/poverty- inequality/what-pay-ratios-in-nifty50-companies-tell-us-about-income-inequality-in-india.html .

Mezzadri, Alessandra and Ravi Srivastava. 2015. 'Labour Regimes in the Indian garment sector: Capital-labour relations, social reproduction and labour standards in the National Capital Region'. Report of ESRC-DFID Research Project, *Labour Standards and the Working Poor in China and India*. Centre for Development Policy and Research.

Mohapatra, Prabhu. 2015. 'Unravelling the puzzle'. *Seminar*. http://www.india-seminar.com/2015/669/669_prabhu_mohapatra.htm .

Mukerjee, Madhusree. 2010. *Churchill's Secret War*. Basic Books.

Nayyar, Mishika; Arushi Chawla; Ayush Pagaria; Ruchi Shukla, 2020. 'The Textile and Apparel Industry: The Change Agent of India'. InvestIndia.Gov.In, July.

Peoples' Union for Democratic Rights. 2017. *Accidents, Death, Repression and Unionisation in SPM Autocomp Systems Pvt. Ltd, Manesar*.

Peoples' Union for Democratic Rights. 2021. *The Anti-Labour Codes: Capitalising a Disaster*.

Perspectives. 2009. *Harvesting Despair: Agrarian Crisis in India*.

Rajadhyaksha, Niranjan. 2020. 'The Indian economic recovery seems led by profits, not wages'. *Mint*. 1 December.

Research Unit For Political Economy. 2005. 'How "Labour Reforms" are implemented: The story of OTIS Elevators', *Aspects of India's Economy*. Nos 39 & 40.

Research Unit For Political Economy. 2012. 'Behind the Present Wave of Unrest in the Auto Sector'. *Aspects of India's Economy*, no. 52.

Research Unit For Political Economy. 2018. 'India's Working Class and Its Prospects: Studies, Reports, Notes, Part I'. *Aspects of India's Economy*, Nos 70 & 71.

Roychowdhury, Anamitra and Kingshuk Sarkar. 2021: 'Labour Reforms in a Neoliberal Setting: Lessons from India'. *Global Labour Journal*, 2021, 12(1)

Roychowdhury, Anamitra. 2018. *Labour Law Reforms in India: All in the name of jobs*. Routledge.

Shastree, Aniruddh. 'Evolution of Minimum Wages Act 1948'. legalserviceindia.com.

Suresh, Haripriya and Prajwal Bhat. 2021. 'Months after H&M factory workers laid off in Karnataka, company to rehire them'. *The News Minute*. 16 February.

Thomas, Jayan Jose. 2019. 'How to Revive Indian Manufacturing? On the Need for Industrial Policy'. *State of Working India*. CSE, Azim Premji University.

Times of India. 2021. 'India has third highest number of billionaires in world: Forbes'. Updated 8 April. https://timesofindia.indiatimes.com/business/india-business/india-has-third-highest-number-of-billionaires-in-world-forbes-rich-list/articleshow/81950980.cms .

Tiwari Anshuman. 2020. 'Falling Through the Cracks: How overlapping responsibilities among many agencies contributes to the poor living conditions of garment workers in Gurgaon, India'. *Berkley Public Policy Journal*. Spring.

Venkat T., Srividya Tadepalli, Thomas Manuel. 2017. 'The Life of Labour: Maruti Suzuki Violence in Manesar – a Retrospective'. *The Wire*, 19 March.

World Bank Group. 2020. *Doing Business 2020: Comparing Business Regulation in 190 economies*.

Yadav, Anumeha. 2015. 'Maruti Strikes'. *Himal Southasian*. March.

ARCHANA AGGARWAL
teaches Economics at Hindu College, University of Delhi.
As a teacher and a student of Economics for more than two
decades, she has been most interested in the question of how
the processes of economic development and India's structural
transformation affect the lives, livelihoods and rights of ordinary
people. This has been the departure point of her academic and
research engagement over many years. Her socially engaged
scholarship has been reflected in her writings for the *Economic
and Political Weekly* and also in her founding of a research
group with university students called *Perspectives*. The group
remained active at the University of Delhi from 2007 to 2014 and
conducted field surveys and brought out reports on issues such as
agrarian distress and labour regimes. Archana has been visiting
different industrial sites within the NCR for nearly a decade and
interacting with workers, managers, contractors and labour rights
activists. These observations and the analysis have now found a
home in the form of the present book.

9 789392 018046